Putting Artificial Intelligence to Work

Evaluating & Implementing Business Applications

Related Titles of Interest from John Wiley & Sons, Inc.

Artificial Intelligence Programming with Turbo Prolog, Weiskamp & Hengl

Expert Systems: Artificial Intelligence in Business, Harmon & King

Expert Systems: Tools and Applications, Harmon, Maus & Morrissey

Programming Expert Systems in Pascal, Sawyer & Foster

Programming Expert Systems in Modula-2, Sawyer & Foster

File Formats for Popular PC Software: A Programmer's Reference, Walden

More File Formats for Popular PC Software: A Programmer's Reference, Walden

Pascal Applications for the Sciences, Crandall

IBM Personal System/2: A Business Perspective, Hoskins

Putting Artificial Intelligence to Work

Evaluating & Implementing Business Applications

Seymour Schoen
Wendell G. Sykes

John Wiley & Sons, Inc.
New York • Chichester • Brisbane • Toronto • Singapore

Trademarks

IBM and IBM PC are registered trademarks of International Business
         Machines, Inc.
Macintosh is a trademark of Apple Computer, Inc.
Polaroid is a registered trademark of Polaroid Corporation
UNIX is a trademark of AT&T

Publisher: Stephen Kippur
Editor: Therese A. Zak
Managing Editor: Ruth Greif
Electronic Book Production Services: Publishers Network

This publication is designed to provide accurate and authoritative information in
regard to the subject matter covered. It is sold with the understanding that the
publisher is not engaged in rendering legal, accounting, or other professional
service. If legal advise or other expert assistance is required, the services of a
competent professional person should be sought. FROM A DECLARATION OF
PRINCIPLES JOINTLY ADOPTED BY A COMMITTEE OF THE AMERICAN BAR
ASSOCIATION AND A COMMITTEE OF PUBLISHERS.

Library of Congress Cataloging-in-Publication Data

Schoen, Seymour.
    Putting artificial intelligence to work.

    1. Artificial intelligence. I. Sykes, Wendell G.
II.   Title.
Q335.S4114 1988   006.3   87-15940
ISBN 0-471-85704-1

Printed in the United States of America
87 88 10 9 8 7 6 5 4 3 2 1

TO ESTHER AND BETSY

Preface

The idea for this book first developed as a result of our experiences while giving talks on artificial intelligence. Initially, the authors did not anticipate the type of questions most frequently posed by the audience. These questions were not of a technical nature, such as the architecture of a knowledge system or its reasoning methodology. Rather, the questions were broader and addressed managerial issues.

What is more, these questions did not come from a particular type of industry or organizational entity. They were asked by people from both long-established and new companies, from government and service organizations, from functional elements such as marketing, engineering, and manufacturing as well as from various levels of management. A frequently expressed viewpoint: "There's a wealth of information (both good and bad) about the promise of AI and how to design a prototype system; we need guidance on if and how to effectively use this technology for real and profitable applications."

Representative questions were:

1. How did you get started?
2. What was your organizational structure?

3. How did you analyze AI's features and limitations?

4. What is entailed in determining return on investment?

5. How do you sell an AI project?

6. How do you select an application?

7. How do you fit it into the way your company does business?

8. How do you organize and manage a project?

The objective of this book is to answer these questions and to respond to the needs of the decision makers who must authorize the capital investment and resources required for a successful project. We aim to offer a balanced evaluation of claims that have been made about the potential and actual value of artificial intelligence technology. The book is also intended to advise and support the "champion" whose role is vital in selling any project involving new technology and sustaining its momentum. Since their role in project success is also important, a discussion of the responsibilities of project engineers and managers for implementing and managing an AI project from inception to field support is presented. Another purpose is to inform individuals who are involved in analyzing technology and its business implications. Finally, we hope to provide students and academic researchers some illumination on the seeming idiosyncracies of the commercial world. The material we present is nearly all based on our own experience. Some of our experiences are presented as anecdotes which highlight the very real issues facing desicion makers and implementers. In some cases, it has been necessary to be less specific than we might wish to protect the security of potential valuable commercial applications.

Since both of us started giving talks about our experiences with and ideas about AI, and particularly while the book was being written, the field of AI has matured considerably. Some of the more enthusiastic predictions have been tempered with reality. The technology investigation/evaluation market has almost disappeared and the suppliers of AI technology are dealing with a market that is solution-oriented and technology-indifferent. The profit and loss sheets of many AI firms certainly reflect this change. A manager dealing with this market must assess the use of AI as a component of an overall computer application strategy, not just as an isolated technology. There is less current experience available for the user of AI under these conditions. Where possible, we have attempted to project our own experience into this new more mature application area to provide guidance for the manager entering it.

A specific effort has been made to avoid extensive discussions of the technical aspects of designing systems. An overview is presented of AI technology which discusses terminology, the representation of knowledge and its manipulation, problem solving and other concepts. For a more detailed understanding of concepts and implementations, the reader should see the references cited for each chapter. Also, for purposes of explanation, the examples presented do not represent the entire range of what is generally considered to be artificial intelligence. Robotics, machine vision and natural language all utilize AI; however, most of the examples used in this book refer to knowledge engineering which has had the most extensive application of AI technology.

Successful development projects are almost always contingent upon good management. Experienced managers will recognize time-honored management precepts in these pages and how they relate to investment and business analysis, planning, staffing, fiscal and schedule control, etc. However, what needs to be understood are the similarities and differences in managing AI and other computer-based technologies. AI deals in complexities, uncertainties, and frequently ill-structured applications unique to this technology. It impacts organizations and their functions. Managers and development personnel must also deal with the added factor of rapidly expanding theoretical foundations upon which very practical AI systems are based. To this must be added the vital experiences gained in developing other computer system.

In writing this book, we did not attempt to redescribe the field of AI as this has been done well by a number of authors, many of whom are cited. Also, since this book is based primarily on our own experiences, we have not covered all aspects of the field of AI with equal depth. Our focus in this book is on the application of AI technology to the support and capturing of knowledge-intensive human activity. We have given less attention to the fields of robotics, advanced AI concepts and natural language since our experience is less relevant and the nature of the applications are different.

To provide an introduction, the book briefly describes the evolution of AI. Also presented are overviews of AI principles and applications. A distinctive feature of the book is a discussion of the concept of knowledge as an organizational resource and how to manage it. The pervasive and sometimes subtle AI impact on business is considered from several viewpoints. Also noted are social and legal implications which may result from incorporating this technology.

We have also attempted to provide an objective account of current and projected features and limitations of AI technology. Remaining chapters of the book are devoted to management issues: investment analysis, selection of an application, selling the project, design responsibility alternatives, implementing and managing the project and other considerations. The sometimes contentious issues of hardware and software choices are discussed, since they can affect other decisions. Finally, there is a description of an actual case history of how this technology was introduced at a large industrial corporation. An extensive list of references cited is also included. Most of the citations are to professional journals and conferences, since the field is moving so rapidly.

The implementation of a new technology requires foresight, patience and ingenuity by both managers and performers. The insights that the authors have gained and attempted to present in this book have been gathered from our own experiences, our colleagues, and those we have encountered in our professional lives. It is impossible for us to acknowledge fully the sources of insight and knowledge that we have used. One of us has been a member of the AI Center at Arthur D. Little, Inc. since its formation. Ideas about the application of AI technology to industrial problems, the market for this technology and the management of knowledge are the joint contribution of all the members of the Center. As authors, we have attempted to structure these ideas, in combination with our experiences, in a form that makes them most useful to managers and decision makers. The other author, in his role as corporate program manager for AI, has received strong support from executives at Litton Industries. Charles S. Bridge, Vice President and Chief Scientist, provided unwavering support and advice from the inception of the program. Orion L. Hoch, President and Fred W. O'Green, Chairman of the Board, provided financial support and encouraged the creation of an environment conducive to evaluating and introducing this technology. The authors also thank Illie Seagren, who prepared manuscripts and did much of the West Coast/East Coast coordination. Finally, we wish to acknowledge the encouragement and tolerance of our families.

Sy Schoen
Beverly Hills, CA

Wendell Sykes
Cambridge, MA

Contents

1

History and Role

THE GROWTH OF ARTIFICIAL INTELLIGENCE

Research

Some three decades ago, research into what is now considered to be Artificial Intelligence (AI) was initiated by some of the first workers with advanced computers who were attempting to use these machines to emulate some aspects of human intelligence with computer software. Since these workers were more interested in computer science than in linguistics, philosophy or logic, some of the efforts were learning experiences in the human sciences for the participants. Thus the AI literature, published and unpublished, is full of descriptions of such learning experiences.

There is a story that in the early days of research on speech understanding, a conference was called to exchange ideas and report progress among the workers in the field. One of the senior attendees offered to bet $50 that no one in the audience could give more than five rules of English grammar.

As has frequently been described, the field of artificial intelligence, or at least the name, was created at a summer conference in 1956 at Dartmouth College that was organized by Marvin Minsky, John McCarthy and Claude Shannon. Most of the research that followed this conference was carried out in academic institutions and government laboratories on a combination of theoretical and practical applications.

Some of the topics investigated were methods of solving problems, written language translation, speech recognition and learning systems. The work on language applications was funded by the U.S. Government with the expectation that practical applications would be possible in a short time. In fact, the problems proved to be more complex than expected and were well beyond the computing power available at the time. Although further work was abandoned for nearly two decades, on these specific topics, some of the techniques to support this research that were developed at the time are still in use for many types of AI systems.

One of the first successful applications of AI was in the field of chemical spectroscopic analysis. Work by Joshua Lederberg in 1964 led to the establishment of the DENDRAL program at Stanford University under the direction of Edward Feigenbaum. Over the next ten years, the DENDRAL system was developed. This system proved to have practical application in the interpretation of mass spectra and has led to a commercial product (Barr and Feigenbaum, 1981).

Another successful program was developed at the Massachusetts Institute of Technology by Engelman, Martin and Moses. This program, MACSYMA, can solve integral equations with at least the capability of a second-year calculus student. It is now a commercial product available on several types of computers (Barr and Feigenbaum, 1981). It should be noted that both DENDRAL and MACSYMA required at least a decade of development and 20–40 person-years of work to complete.

Several other research programs in various fields, including medicine and biology, have led to the development of expert system shells that are now sold commercially by companies formed specifically for this purpose.

Role of government

The fact that a substantial body of AI research has been performed and that there are now several generations of trained AI researchers is almost entirely due to the support of the Federal Government, primarily the Defense Department and the National Science Foundation. The Defense Advanced Research Projects Agency has provided continuing support for AI research in academic institutions and other groups in the face of a sometimes discouraging lack of immediate practical results. In the last several years, there has been a dramatic increase in interest in the use of AI in the more operationally oriented parts of the Federal Government and nearly every major Government institution has attempted to apply this technology to some of its significant problems. Both the Strategic Defense Initiative and the Strategic Computing Program have made major investments in this area.

Venture capital

An important factor in the explosive growth of the AI applications industry has been the role of venture capital in supporting the burgeoning growth of AI start-up companies that began about 1980. It seems that the interest in AI started to pick up at about the same time that increasing amounts of venture capital funds were becoming available. The pressure for AI investment grew to a point where nearly all of the leading figures in the AI world had formed their own companies, each engaged in selling some form of AI-related hardware or software. Since many of the purchasers of AI products were looking for hardware and software to support their own development work on initial systems, these companies usually found a ready market for their products.

Application

In the past few years, there has been a great deal of activity in the development of applications of AI by both industry and government. The result has been a general recognition that the technology has real potential value and it seems likely that a second wave of application development, focused on problem solution rather than technology investigation, is about to start. Since the objectives and financial justification requirements are somewhat different for solution-oriented applications, it is quite likely that this second wave will require changes in technology and marketing methods for those firms that wish to participate to any considerable extent.

One of the problems that a manager, attempting to evaluate the promise of AI for this second wave will have, is the lack of discrimination that has existed in the literature between descriptions of research projects that have attempted to demonstrate the potential of a new technology and operational systems that are actually providing profitable results to their developers. Much of the literature has focused on reporting both types in the same manner, thus making it difficult for an inexperienced reader to discriminate between them. For a considerable period of time, R1/XCON was frequently used as an example of an operational system, probably because it was the only significant system in daily use. Other systems that were described in the literature as "operational" proved to be far from such a condition. Most of the systems that were described were actually prototypes that proved to require a large amount of additional resources and time to reach "operational" status. Thus, much of the material provided in the literature did not have a great deal of relevance to the actual problems of converting a new technology into a profitable and operational system. The actual focus was more on the initial phase of a technology evaluation designed to determine whether the substantial investment required to utilize this technology was actually worthwhile.

As a number of companies have completed their evalutions and embarked on serious use of the technology, a new problem has become obvious. The development cycle for an operational system is much longer and so there is not as much published information available because most systems are (1987) still under development. Also, the development and integration problems for an operational system are different. Many of the problems have apparently little to do with AI as such but rather are associated with the interface between a new technology and the more prosaic problems of interfacing with existing systems and technology. There is an obvious reason why these problems have not been fully addressed at this stage in the maturation cycle of AI technology. We have found that it is usually as expensive to provide a real-world interface to a prototype as it is to build the prototype itself. Thus in a technology evaluation mode, it was not cost-effective to devote limited resources to integration since it seemed that such work was relatively low-risk.

The major companies that are actively using AI in their operations are reluctant to publish the results because of the competitive advantage that might be lost if the results were known. In writing this book, we have attempted to use examples from our own experience to provide insight into some of the successes and problems we have encountered to compensate for this missing but important information.

One factor we wish to emphasize is that, although rapid methods of developing prototypes ("Rapid Prototyping") derived from AI system development technology have made it possible to create a demonstration system in a short time, there is no experience that would indicate that the development and maintenance of a large and complex AI system is any easier than a more conventional system of equal size. In fact, the opposite may be true because of the complex interactions that are possible within a rule-based system. AI technology can offer real benefit to the user, but not all the problems have yet been solved.

Another factor is the strong focus in most of the literature on the rule-based expert system, to the point where it may seem that AI and rule-based expert systems are synonymous. An expert system is a computer program designed to represent knowledge of a particular subject as provided by a human expert or other source of information. The system also includes procedures for utilizing this knowledge to arrive at a solution to a problem of the type which would normally require human expertise. In actual fact, there are a considerable number of applications of artificial intelligence technology that are different from the classic "Expert System." Some of these applications will be discussed in this book. As an example, it is easier to develop an "intelligent assistant" that can take over some of the routine aspects of the work of an expert, thus freeing him or her to focus on areas where expert knowledge is truly needed in a form that is difficult to provide with current software technology.

An example of a different branch of AI is the augmentation of vision systems. Such systems are used for industrial inspection, combining a representation of subjective human judgment and feature recognition techniques for edges, texture or contrast differences. Natural language systems that attempt to provide computerized equivalents for some aspects of the human ability to extract information by listening to speech or reading text have been used to recognize simple spoken or typed commands and extract information from digitized text.

Future

Several surprising trends may occur in the types of AI technology that will be developed and used in the near future. There will be a rapidly growing use of small and imbedded AI-based systems in conventional software programs. These systems will improve the utility of large, conventional programs and reduce the training requirements for their use.

We also expect that there will be a trend away from large, general-purpose software programs used for the development of AI applications. Instead, suppliers of these types of programs will focus on modular components that can be easily customized into an application-specific system. It seems likely that only such modularization will permit the building and maintenance of complex systems as computers, operating systems, languages and program development components are upgraded and debugged.

It seems unlikely that decision making under uncertainty capabilities of the human will be replaced by software in the near future. Rather the focus will be on enriching the decision-making environment of humans and in improving the quality and uniformity of more routine decision making. The next major leap in capability will most likely occur when our ability to write software that can utilize massive parallelism matches our current ability to build it.

VIEWS OF AI

AI as enabling technology

This section provides a high-level overview of the state and use of AI technology that may be of assistance to the reader in following some of the ideas presented in later sections of this book.

We feel that it is important to understand the major potential applications of AI in order to interpret what has happened in the past and what may happen in the near future.

In many publications, AI has been described as a revolutionary science that will change the nature of almost any area to which it is applied. To a considerable extent, these descriptions have been based on extrapolations of the research projects that have been undertaken to understand, by attempts at implementation in a computer, the nature of human intelligence. In reality, there may be a considerable distance between the stated goal of a research program to prove that a concept might be possible, and an operating software and hardware system that provides a profitable service for its user. In some of the earlier descriptions of the potential for AI, this distinction was not clearly made. It is probably more realistic to think of AI as providing an enabling technology that permits the building of certain types of computer-based software systems that have been difficult or impossible to develop in the past. Careful application of the techniques of knowledge elicitation and analysis can also lead to improved insight into the requirements for the utilization of knowledge in an organization.

To take a somewhat simplified view of the field of AI as it has been implemented in the last few years, the primary focus of users has been on the evaluation of the technology. This focus has resulted in both application development and sales of hardware and software appropriate for technology evaluation. The majority of users of the technology have been development groups, formed for the specific purpose of implementing AI applications, often supported with research and development funds. These groups have focused on the implementation of applications that served the dual purpose of meeting an important corporate need and demonstrating the value of AI technology. The manufacturers of AI hardware and software have been selling into this market and perhaps believe that this market will continue and will grow at the rate that has been predicted for the overall number of knowledge workers. It is not clear that this belief is justified. This possibility has some importance to a manager who may be considering a commitment to a particular technology for a long-term application. It is well to be sure that the supplier of the technology will be available for support for the expected lifetime of his or her product.

Another factor that the manager of a technology evaluation program should consider is the natural tension between a sponsor of a technology evaluation and the ultimate user, especially if both are funding the program. It may well be that the most important objectives of the user can be satisfied without AI technology and the most interesting applications of AI may be of minor value to the user. The recognition of the existence of this tension, and its resolution, should be an important management objective. The most effective method for tension resolution and, for that matter, for facilitation of the system design process may be to make explicit the goals and objectives of each of the participants in the design process at the start. If there is a conflict in objectives due to the nature of the interim results of the system-design process, the participants can negotiate under conditions where their interests are explicit. Setting of project goals is more fully discussed in Chapter 12.

Examples of some questions that might be asked of the participants in the process of application selection and system design are:

1. What are the relative priorities between evaluating new technologies and solving the problem to which these technologies are to be applied?

2. How carefully has the overall task of the user in performing his or her job been considered in the system design?

It is possible that the general understanding of and experience with the use of AI technology in the potential user community has matured to a point where most new applications that use AI technology will be funded from sources that are problem-solution oriented, not technology oriented, and that the firms that offer problem solutions will dominate the marketplace. This conclusion has some interesting implications for both manufacturers of AI technology and for system developers. For example, we found several AI systems suggested for development that were to be used in an area where a large and conventional data-base management system was also under development. In each case, this conventional system was described by its developers as "solving" a number of long-term and difficult problems which were critical to the health or growth of the mainline business of the corporation. The ultimate solution had been delayed for some time; an AI technology solution was accepted as a short-term measure because it was offered as an enhancement that might possibly be useful to the operational entity that had been long waiting for the true solution.

Those firms that will survive in the new market will be those that offer AI technology as a component of a complete solution, not as an isolated technology. For the manager interested in using AI technology in the long term, integration with conventional technology is probably as important as location is for real estate.

Return to the craftsman

Just before he died, Dr. Joseph Harrington, the father of Computer Integrated Manufacturing (CIM), gave an informal talk on his latest view of the future of automation in manufacturing. One of the authors was privileged to attend this talk. Because of its pertinence to the topic of this book, the main ideas are repeated here. Figure 1.1 identifies the changes in the nature of the primary

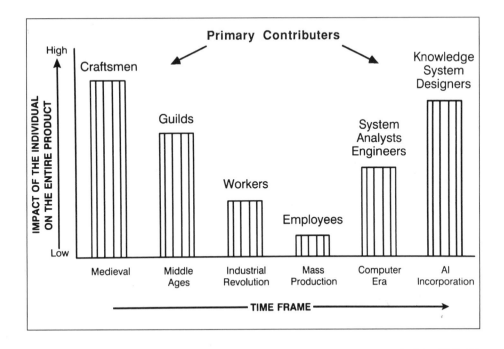

Figure 1.1
Individual Contributions

contributors to manufactured products. In the Middle Ages, the primary contributor was a craftsman who was simultaneously a designer, a salesman, a manufacturer and a repairman. A smith might design a suit of armour for a knight, forge the parts himself and maintain the suit for its useful lifetime. An apprentice learned the smith's trade from the smith in return for his supervised labor on components of the product. However, the final product was uniquely the result of the ideas of a single individual.

As Guilds evolved in the Middle Ages, there was increasing specialization of skills within a trade, but the master craftsman was still the primary source of inspiration and management for the entire product cycle. During the Industrial Revolution, manufacturing became more a piecework operation and the role of the master craftsman was fragmented among a large number of specialized practitioners, each of whom had only a limited view of the entire process. As the capability of design-related AI systems increases, it will be again possible for the designer to have an overall view of the entire process and resume the role of the master craftsman.

2

Potential for Artificial Intelligence

BASIS FOR THE POTENTIAL

What is the essential difference between existing computer science and what is called "AI"? What is the basis for the widespread interest in the subject today? These are difficult but legitimate questions which may be asked by anyone considering an investment of resources in developing or incorporating AI technology.

A primary feature of most AI applications is an attempt to utilize formal and informal human knowledge in a structured way. The expected potential of AI technology is based on increasing the availability and usefulness of expert knowledge. It is this potential which will affect many diverse areas: education, commerce, government, medicine and manufacturing. (A representative listing of potential applications is presented in Chapter 3.) Additionally, this technology is being used to enhance the understanding of human thought processes and is facilitating the generation of new knowledge. Features and limitations of AI technology are discussed in Chapter 4.

CAPTURING KNOWLEDGE

One of the most important results of work on artificial intelligence in the last few years has been a refinement of techniques for obtaining and structuring the knowledge of experts. These techniques are discussed at length in Chapter 7. This refinement has come because of the requirement for extreme precision in the definition of procedures and knowledge when implementing them in a computer program. There are a number of short- and long-term benefits associated with the use of such techniques. There are many islands of expertise, scattered throughout industry, containing knowledge that is an essential part of business resources. When labor costs were low and employment relatively stable it was possible to use the apprenticeship method to capture and transfer this knowledge from generation to generation. Under present conditions, apprenticeship is not as applicable because new technology is being introduced into the workplace and the old knowledge must be integrated with this technology. As the older workers retire, their knowledge and experience is lost permanently before it can be used with new technology.

We believe, therefore, that capturing knowledge should be a significant priority for corporate America. The strong interest in building expert systems has tended to obscure the fact that capturing knowledge for reuse in a new way can be a goal in itself and should be evaluated as such. It may well be that, as new technology is introduced, elements of the old knowledge may be restructured and imbedded in a new system rather than being captured in its present complete state in a computerized system.

An interesting example might be the knowledge of an expert machinist who is capable of doing high-precision work on existing machinery. His knowledge of materials, tool shape, feed rates, lubricants and the sound and sight of the machining process can be captured and used in automatic machines that can do the same work at lower cost.

In a number of cases, the knowledge elicitation that was to precede the development of an expert system revealed that a computerized solution to the problem was found to be essentially unnecessary. Training or procedural changes provided the most cost-effective solution.

When starting the selection of an application and the initial knowledge elicitation associated with it, the manager should be alert to the possibility that computerization may not be necessary. As long as real benefits are achieved, the specific method used to attain them is not important. If, as is often true at present, the purpose of the development of an AI system is to demonstrate the value of the technology as a beginning of a corporate effort to use the technology on a large scale, the developer should make it clear that one possible result of a particular project may actually be a noncomputerized solution. The developer should also make it clear that such a result should not be taken as a failure, but rather as proof that the technology can offer a wide range of possible benefits depending on the solution. Because of the potential benefit, we believe that knowledge-elicitation technology will become an accepted part of human-resources technology and will be employed over a wide range of applications.

Focused and intensive use of knowledge-elicitation technology is particularly appropriate in areas where much of the knowledge is based on direct experience over an extended time with processes or operations where simple algorithmic logic does not really apply. Specific examples of such processes are found in chemical plants, machining operations, forecasting and prediction, and in initial system design.

As is discussed in greater detail elsewhere, one of the most effective methods of capturing knowledge that can be automated is with a semi-operational prototype. Such a prototype, if well designed, produces an immediate improvement in the work environment of the expert. Thus, the expert receives direct benefit for further participation in the elicitation process while simultaneously providing additional knowledge to the elicitor who can observe the expert at work in a structured environment that directly supports observation and restructuring.

A prototype can even be used for creative knowledge development. If a new, computer-based capability is created that is intended to be automated but the knowledge to support this automation does not currently exist, it seems logical to create a simulation that will permit a human operator to emulate the process to be automated and then capture this knowledge as the basis for final system design.

ENHANCING EXISTING PRACTICE

There are several specific examples of the type of benefits that can be obtained from the use of knowledge-capture techniques. One benefit that has been observed is the creation of a "language" that greatly improves the ability to transmit information under conditions where such transmission was not previously possible. The knowledge elicitor must, of necessity, create such a language which may include both a symbol set and a representational structure.

A knowledge elicitor, working on a diagnostic system for a chemical plant designed to avoid serious plant upsets, created a knowledge representation language for the design process based on three simple symbols. This language was immediately accepted by the plant operators as a primary means of communication. Further, the two most skilled operators, in a day of intense activity, created about 150 rule sets that contained nearly all their accumulated knowledge in this language.

There is a wide range of technology that has been developed to support the implementation of AI applications. As the technology drives down the price-performance curve, it becomes increasingly attractive to use it in non-AI applications. Specific examples are the rich graphical interfaces that can be constructed with relative ease, the ability to present complex control structures that has already become commonplace in the Macintosh computer and the various techniques for the representation of and access to information.

There is a general class of what might be called mini-applications of AI that can be used to raise the level of performance of a group of information workers of varying skill levels. If there are components of the common tasks that can benefit from either reminding or automation, these mini-applications can be used as performance enhancers for the workers of lower skill level.

As knowledge analysis is performed, it may become obvious that the best system solution may not be a simple replacement but rather a combination of automation and human effort that improves an existing either totally manual implementation or a lower degree of automation that is not directed toward development of a higher common capability.

The sophisticated designer of computer systems is probably asking "so what's new?" at this point. Our answer is that the impact of many applications of AI technology is only a matter of degree.

A STRUCTURE AND LANGUAGE FOR DIALOG

As we have been part of the construction of various expert systems, we have come to believe that considerable importance should be given to using a communication structure for user interaction that is congruent with the knowledge and communication of the user. We feel that such matching will become even more important as the use of computers is extended into areas where computer literacy has not been expected or common. We have found that if we can make the user interface contain symbols and logical structure that match those of the user that the perceived value of the system seems much higher.

THE TRANSPARENT INTERFACE

The term "user friendly" has been freely applied to many software user interfaces where varying amounts of attention have been given to the design of the interface by the developer of the software. We believe that true "user friendliness" can be described as presenting an interface that seems intuitively natural, that does not require an instruction manual or training and that does not cause frequent errors in use. Using the techniques of knowledge engineering, described in Chapter 7 and the "rapid prototyping" technology described in Chapters 4 and 11, we believe that it is possible to design and construct a user interface that comes close to this ideal. It is important to use representation methods that are close to the thought patterns of the user, symbols and words that have the correct meaning in the context where they are used and logical structures that match the mental organization of the user.

It is clear at this stage in the development of such interfaces that it is possible to meet the goals stated above for an individual expert. It is less clear that a more general and less personal interface will be as effective. If not, it seems possible to build an interface with a very high level command language for a particular area that will permit customization by individual users. The idea of customization by high-level languages extends beyond the static situation described above. It is likely that most users will change their work patterns over time and require continued change in their work interface. Thus, a high level command language will support updating of the interface to maintain peak performance.

Such command languages, in less user friendly form, are already available in many popular personal computer (PC) software packages. Thus, we are describing an evolutionary, not a revolutionary, change. As available computer power increases, it may be possible to provide an interface that observes the pattern of consistent errors and either self-corrects or at least suggests the nature of programming changes that might be needed. Performance monitoring systems are already in use for applications where large numbers of operators perform repetitive tasks. It may not be long before such systems can be made supportive, rather than punitive.

TOOLS FOR NON-AI APPLICATIONS

Much of the technology associated with the so called "high-end" AI development tools were provided for programmers who were attempting to develop and debug large and complex AI programs. The same tools should be equally useful, if available at lower cost, for more conventional programming. The continued decline in the cost of high-power workstations should make it possible to provide code development environments that will assist the programmer to provide correct code syntax and visualize the flow of logical control in ways that will improve the speed and quality of developed code.

IMPACT ON BUSINESS

Decision making

The combination of AI technology and the availability of high-power and low-cost personal computers will have a major impact on many aspects of present-day American industry. This impact has been delayed by the difficulty of using computational assistance without also devoting considerable effort to "learning" to use computers and adapting an existing style of work to a relatively inflexible computing technology. Only after a decade has computer-based word processing become commonplace although the basic technology has been available, at rapidly decreasing cost, for about 15 years.

AI technology, when properly applied, will reduce the slow software development cycle that seems to lag behind the availability of hardware by at least five years. When proper capability is available, the manner in which employees perform their jobs, how these jobs are assigned, the management decision process and the overall perception of work will be changed.

Recent work on the use of AI in management decision making has provided a preliminary view of the nature of the change. Consider, for example, the characteristics of the environment in which there must be an action by a decision maker, as illustrated in Figure 2.1. Some of the factors of importance are relevance, timeliness, and reliability of the information. Frequently, a total or best answer is not required, or may not even be possible. For example, the need for making a timely decision or the requirement for obtaining even more data precludes getting a complete or optimum solution.

As with human experts, no knowledge system that can be built today can always provide an unequivocal answer or one with a high degree of certainty in all cases where it is used. Human experts also express themselves inexactly—"this *usually* is true" or "this will *probably* happen." Furthermore, definitions of these terms may not be universally true or acceptable over the total range of possibilities. In many cases, the problem is not in making the decision but rather in obtaining sufficient information on which to make a reasonable decision. The expert knowledge lies in the method used to obtain data and the analysis process to be performed on it. In such cases, the optimum decision-support system is one that can provide the information to support the decision, not to make it. A decision-support system that meets this requirement would appear as an intelligent staff assistant that presented the pertinent information in a condensed and understandable form, not as a black box that makes decisions. In fact, the dividing line between an easy to use data-base system and an expert decision support system may not be distinct.

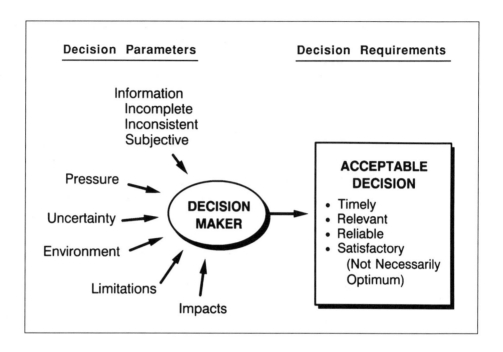

Figure 2.1
Decision-making Environment

In more structured situations, it may be possible for the system to select a "satisfactory" answer or present a set of alternatives and the implications of their use that the decision-maker can select from.

There is continuing research on the use of AI technology to assist managers in nonquantifiable areas (Jordan, 1986). Knowledge systems are being evaluated that can provide answers to such subjective questions as:

- What's really the problem?

- How does all this fit together?

- What does common sense tell me?

Pressure may also be an element of the decision-making environment, as depicted in Figure 2.1. This pressure may be caused by the economic or political implications of the decision, life-threatening possibilities or other consequences which cannot be foreseen at the time. For example, some have theorized that the need for making decisions under a great deal of pressure with masses of rapidly occurring sensor input contributed to the disaster at Three Mile Island. A less catastrophic but increasingly serious problem as factories become more automated is the occurrence of a major upset in some part of the production process. An operator, faced with the need to consider input from a hundred sensors in but a few minutes, may reasonably conclude that the safest course is to shut down the process. However, the apparent major upset could really be a false alarm and the shutdown could cost thousands of dollars.

Another example would be the production planner who must quickly make changes in the production schedule or be faced with the prospect of idle people on the assembly line. In each of these examples, a valuable adjunct would be a knowledge system which could assist in the rapid diagnosis of the problem and support the selection of alternatives by a human operator.

Other elements of the decision-making environment may entail a great deal of uncertainty, intuition, or hunches. Consider the situation of an experienced shop foreman who says that "On warm summer afternoons, I do not assign work on milling machine 3." If questioned as to why he does not make that particular assignment on summer afternoons, he eventually explains that the machine goes out of tolerance, but admits he cannot determine the cause. As the capability of knowledge systems continues to increase, they will be able to provide valuable assistance to decision makers who must rely on intuition or respond under a great deal of pressure.

Another managerial area in which knowledge systems are being applied in increasing numbers involves their assistance to managers. Typically, managers are responsible for expensive or scarce resources. They are faced with the need for making many trade-offs and being responsive to numerous criteria, some of which are conflicting (Bimson and Burris, 1986). Knowledge-based systems can go considerably beyond the capability of spreadsheets in providing the manager with alternatives and their consequences.

Another potential benefit of knowledge systems is the improvement of decentralized decision making. As the appropriate information and access to that information is made available at additional levels of the organization, it becomes increasingly feasible to delegate decision making to an optimum location. Delegation of responsibility for decisions can be based on management considerations rather than the difficulty of providing information upon which to base a good decision. This delegation of authority requires a satisfactory flow of information through the enterprise, which can be supported with the use of AI technology. A knowledge system can be designed to contain information and decision rules appropriate to various processes and transactions. An example is the many steps entailed in ordering material from a supplier and processing it through receiving inspection, stocking, accounts payable, inventory, etc. The knowledge system can provide flexible assistance to users who provide input at each of these steps. In a complex business environment, it is difficult to satisfy all of the indicated constraints and preferences on how the work is to be performed. AI methodologies are being introduced to aid in the modeling of these environments and to provide a basis for making compromises between conflicting constraints. For example, in scheduling the flow of work through a factory, how should the conflicting goals of efficient order processing, optimum use of machines, and minimizing work in process be resolved (Smith and Owi, 1986)?

Information handling

For some time, there has been a growing awareness in industry and government of the importance of information to the success of an enterprise. The behavior and methods of operation of most organizations have changed to take advantage of new, computer-based methods of generating and organizing data and information. However, the use of this technology has created large amounts of information. This information is drawn from many sources—both internal and external. Frequently, the information is stored in a variety of data bases, some with incompatible formats and content, which are accessed with different communication networks which further increase the amount of available, but not necessarily usable, information. As a result, there can be too much of a good thing.

It has been suggested that networking individual knowledge systems will provide better interfaces to large data bases and more efficient utilization of peripheral devices. Further advances in technology will permit users of a particular knowledge system to obtain assistance from a different or specialized knowledge base. The individual knowledge systems can be augmented or modified with minimal impact on other organization activities (Tenant, 1986). Also, a system design based on modular components will make it easier to understand the operation and maintain performance of the system as user needs and methods change.

There are many examples where the amount of information available exceeds the human ability to use it effectively. Consider the position of a battlefield commander whose technically sophisticated sensors provide a potentially overwhelming amount of detailed information. The commander and his staff must, somehow, sort and correlate the information to get at what is needed at a particular moment. It is necessary to determine what is relevant and what will have little effect on the decision. A similar problem is faced by the executive who is provided with a high stack of computer printouts filled with economic data that tells little or nothing directly relevant to what is likely to happen to sales in the Northeast region. Knowledge systems with information-screening capability can be effective in limiting the presentation of information to that which is pertinent to and directly supports human intervention.

Another complication in accessing information, which is really not uncommon, is introduced by a individuals desiring computer-based information but really not being sure of what they need or want. The manager wishes to obtain information, located in various employee files, on which to base projections for salary reviews or specialized staffing requirements. This requires the personnel department to interpret the manager's needs and relate them to what is available in the personnel department data bases. The process would be expedited if the manager could work interactively with each data base to obtain partial information to help define his request. Also, the day-long turnarounds that are normal with large batch processing systems are, at least, a source of annoyance. What is required is a system that supports appropriate realtime access and convenient interaction with the data base without the necessity of learning a new and sometimes arcane language and process.

To solve this type of problem, there is great interest in natural language systems which utilize artificial intelligence techniques to provide a human-oriented interface to data bases. A hypothetical example of a dialog with a natural language system is

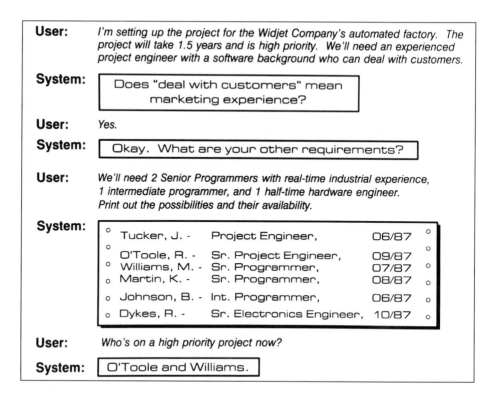

User:	*I'm setting up the project for the Widjet Company's automated factory. The project will take 1.5 years and is high priority. We'll need an experienced project engineer with a software background who can deal with customers.*
System:	Does "deal with customers" mean marketing experience?
User:	*Yes.*
System:	Okay. What are your other requirements?
User:	*We'll need 2 Senior Programmers with real-time industrial experience, 1 intermediate programmer, and 1 half-time hardware engineer. Print out the possibilities and their availability.*
System:	Tucker, J. - Project Engineer, 06/87 O'Toole, R. - Sr. Project Engineer, 09/87 Williams, M. - Sr. Programmer, 07/87 Martin, K. - Sr. Programmer, 08/87 Johnson, B. - Int. Programmer, 06/87 Dykes, R. - Sr. Electronics Engineer, 10/87
User:	*Who's on a high priority project now?*
System:	O'Toole and Williams.

Figure 2.2
Example of Developmental Natural Language System

shown in Figure 2.2. User input and system responses are shown. These systems are designed to support the needs of modern organizations for broad-based rapid communications across departmental lines, enabling different departments to access common data bases in a generally usable format. However, these systems function best in situations where a limited vocabulary can be used and a certain amount of training is possible for most users. When installed, the vocabulary and recognition logic of each system must be tailored for the specific application and retailored if there is any significant change in usage. An intelligent data base assistant has been developed which helps a user formulate his or her inquiry. This system features querying on a conceptual level rather than by specific facts. It locates the data base segment containing the requested information, retrieves it, and presents it to the requestor. The system is intended to be portable to other data bases (Piatetsky-Shapiro *et al.*, 1986).

Natural language front ends provide an alternative to the conventional hierarchy structures where information is distributed in defined sequences. For example, a data base inquiry on shipping container requirements for a particular component may entail working through other data bases relating to engineering, procurement, contracts, marketing, etc. This hierarchy structure becomes even more unwieldy with the increased use of distributed processing. Many individuals now have a personal computer class of machine on their desk, and they require access to information but need to do so without being irritated by computer idiosyncracies. Progress is being made in developing natural language interfaces to PC-based data bases (Seeley *et al.*, 1986).

Engineering

Much effort has gone into structuring data bases to make them more responsive to the needs of their users. A frequent problem is growth in number and size of an organization's data bases. Much of the material in the separate bases is effectively redundant but expressed in different structures and formats. As an example, an original engineering design subsequently spawns new material in data bases used by manufacturing, test, purchasing, receiving inspection, finance, marketing, and so on. These data bases service different needs, yet much of the information in all of these data bases is equivalent. Additionally, in the process of their creation, numerous translation errors may occur.

Recent AI technology based extensions of existing Computer Aided Design and Computer Aided Manufacturing (CAD/CAM) systems are encouraging in that they endeavor to provide some commonality across data bases. Providing natural language interfaces for a central data base that are appropriate to the activities of each design group would further reduce the incentive for creating overlapping (or private) data bases. As CAD/CAM design methods are used in an increasingly automated environment, inconsistent and overlapping data bases become both extremely troublesome and solvable. Simple expert systems can handle either translation or reconciliation so that elements of data entered at one point in the design process can be propagated across other corporate data bases with little effort. Where the existing situation is complex, simple expert systems can be built to assist in the gradual cleanup of old and inconsistent data.

The problem of data cleanup, the protection of mini-empires and the considerable cost associated with a major change in the organization of such fundamental systems as major corporate data bases has slowed serious attention to the resolution of this problem. Its solution however, with the use of AI technology, will remove a significant impediment to increasing the scope of computer-integrated manufacturing in industry.

Combining knowledge systems with existing data bases introduces technical complexity. There is a wide variety of hardware and software protocols for obtaining or adding to information in data bases. A "front-end" knowledge system must be totally compatible with these protocols and require a minimum of overhead processing. Typically, this entails customizing the knowledge system to the format and control structure of a particular data base. Such customizing can be costly, require a high degree of technical understanding, and introduce complexities in maintaining the system. The issue of insuring the security of information in the data base also becomes more complicated. The knowledge system's feature of being able to explain its reasoning makes it easier to compromise data security since the control logic of the system becomes available to the user.

Maintaining proprietary information is also impacted by the increasingly widespread use of computer-integrated manufacturing (CIM) systems. A great deal of vital information must be accessible in a CIM system. AI technology is being utilized to recognize unusual inquiry patterns which might signal an attempt at unauthorized access. The general problem of computer security maintenance can be attacked by the same methods. An AI system that can recognize "unusual" behavior in the operating system can alert an operator to an attempt at penetration.

Knowledge-based systems are improving the handling of information in many types of applications. An interesting example is found in the legal profession. A set of tools, utilizing artificial intelligence technology, has been developed for attorneys. These tools are included in developmental systems which provide much improved menus, communications, a case "briefer" and outliner, a full text data base, a computer-assisted instructional system and an automated law practice system (Sprowl *et al.*, 1986).

Knowledge-based systems can enhance productivity in other areas. When developed, such systems will change the process of software coding and testing, normally an expensive and time consuming process.

AI-based design techniques are being used to develop software productivity tools. When development is completed some of these tools will generate a knowledge base of information about hardware storage and instruction formats, coding techniques, data flow, and interface conventions. Another tool enhances the documentation of an assembly language by providing comments about the action that will occur when each line of code executes (Wolfe, 1986).

The cost and requirements for maintaining software after it has been delivered to the user are an important part of total system cost. More than half of the total resources expended on software during its life cycle go into maintenance. It is expected that the potential capability of knowledge-based systems to assist in storing, documenting, and retrieving information about software will provide an important asset during the maintenance cycle (Anon., 1986).

Another area in which AI technology can increase productivity is in engineering and manufacturing design. A knowledge system, which is interfaced to a CAD/CAM system, can contain knowledge about design procedures and manufacturing processes. It may also be used to match new product requirements with features of previously designed products (Kinoglu *et al.*, 1986). Promising research results have been reported on a system which can even perform some of the more routine engineering design tasks (Mittal *et al.*, 1986).

Systems that can learn from experience are likely to be much farther in the future, although it may be possible to provide a focused and limited capability. Recent work with neural network systems has had encouraging but very preliminary results in demonstrating a learning from experience capability. Since these systems will normally give the closest approximate answer to any input, they should have robust performance in changing conditions. A more attainable capability could be a teachable system that could be easily programmed to recognize a new condition. Consider for example, the potential application of a teachable system in a manufacturing environment. When a particular type of quality control problem begins to recur, what are the most likely causes of the problem? A knowledge system with teachable capability will keep a record of faults as they occur and can be taught to recognize patterns. This pattern recognition can assist the operator to identify likely causes of the problem.

Production operations are increasingly utilizing knowledge systems. These applications are not limited to high volume manufacturing operations such as automobiles. Actually, batch processes predominate in many industries. These processes are characterized by short production runs, many product variations, and frequent changes. Much time must be spent in "white collar" planning. Decision making in such an environment may contain the following elements:

1. Complexity: There may be many interrelationships between people, material, complex testing procedures (including significantly, product liability concerns), and government regulations.

2. Interdependence: Changing a single parameter can cause ripples in many other activities.

3. Short reaction time needs: Schedule pressures, if planning is not timely the production line must be shut down and people are idle.

4. Flexibility: The production process must respond to changing markets, customer input and design changes.

An example of applying AI technology to a batch manufacturing environment is a simulation of a sheet metal fabrication process developed by an aerospace company. The facility produces small quantities of many different parts on various machines. The knowledge system greatly facilitates the analysis of set-up times and selection of jobs from a queue. It devises machine routing strategies and calculates processing time (Faught, 1986).

Companies that have batch manufacturing operations are installing flexible machining systems (FMS) to increase productivity. An FMS essentially consists of a set of machines connected by an automated transportation system. It is designed to adapt rapidly to changes in production mix and volume. Scheduling of an FMS installation is complicated since machine utilization must be optimized while accommodating frequent production changes. As compared to conventional computerized production scheduling, a recently developed expert system is expected to have much greater flexibility and is easier to maintain (Bruno *et al.*, 1986).

Decentralization does not eliminate the need for good communication between elements of the organization. Problems with overall productivity have been found in manufacturing plants where individual "islands of automation" have evolved. The productivity within an island may have improved but the overall production process does not flow smoothly from one "island" to another. Performance might be increased by designing and implementing a system which has knowledge of the input and output of individual processes, the data bases being used in each process and the nature of the interaction between them. The system should provide communication or at least central monitoring of the current state and performance history of each "island." Since "no subprocess is an island," the system should provide a mechanism, based on process interaction knowledge, that will control the interactions between "islands" to prevent overflows and shortages in the components of the overall process.

Advances in manufacturing technology will generate numerous potential applications of AI technology. For example, metal fabricators are increasingly using a variety of difficult to machine high-temperature alloys controlled by computer-integrated manufacturing (CIM) systems. Advanced application-specific tools and methods are required to fabricate these alloys. Knowledge systems are being developed for planning this complex process. Trouble-shooting machinery in a CIM environment is made more difficult by the requirement to understand multiple disciplines: computer hardware and software, communications, electronic sensors and controls, as well as processing and machine technology. Additionally, the source of the problem may be one of gradual performance degradation of the equipment rather than complete breakdown.

Effective maintenance of such installations requires a knowledge of system subtleties as well as interdisciplinary understanding. AI-based diagnostic systems are assisting service personnel to increase the on-line performance of these sophisticated production machines. As further evidence of the potential significance of AI technology to manufacturing, the U.S. Air Force has established an AI Manufacturing Research Center.

Availability of important expertise may also be a problem for the production manager. The labor force is changing. Perhaps it is better educated, but it has no "feel" for the production process. The old time machinist is representative of a vanishing breed who can look at the color of the chips flying off a piece of metal and decide that the cutting tool is becoming dull. Elements of the production environment—flexibility, complexity, dissemination of information, etc.—are all features of knowledge-based systems.

Other production operations have the potential for a good payback from the use of an AI system. There is a great need for more automation and consistency in quality control. The difficulty is that many quality control functions, such as inspection, tend to be nonquantitative. These functions are dependent on inexact conclusions and apparently vague impressions. An example is an inspector who can look at a metal surface and say: "The paint looks O.K." or "It looks like it's got a little ripple in it." Another inspector may look at a solder joint and intuitively be able to tell that too much flux was used in the soldering process without being able to explain the source of that conclusion. Can such intuition and experience be captured in a knowledge-based system? There is much R&D effort being applied to the development of systems which can incorporate this type of uncertainty, experience and intuition.

Putting increasing amounts of high-tech equipment on the factory floor brings a number of other problems with it. Consider the situation of the production foreman who has to maintain many different types of sophisticated equipment. He is sufficiently far-thinking to have sent his maintenance man to several vendor schools each of which has taught this technician how to maintain their own high-tech equipment. Unfortunately, some time after having attended several of these schools, a technician may not remember which information that was learned applies to servicing which type of equipment. Again, an AI-based diagnosis system could be of help in such situations.

There are also situations where manufacturers of complex equipment are being asked to provide knowledge-based diagnosis systems with their equipment. In addition to market forces, government agencies are also imposing demands on product design, particularly as it relates to safety. A highly visible example is the pressure on the nuclear power industry to increase their safety procedures. Knowledge systems are being developed to assist in plant operation and response to emergency conditions. The systems interpret data from many sensors and from external factors such as weather and earthquakes.

Central maintenance service centers are being developed by several companies. They are intended for worldwide access by technicians needing diagnostic assistance or product updates. This has evolved into a new business opportunity for a company which now markets diagnostic services to outside customers. Utilization of these systems will be broadened by the addition of more extensive natural language implementations that may be accessed on a technician's terminal. This approach to remote diagnostics, however, loses some of its utility if specialized test equipment is still required at the site.

Administration and marketing

Increasing worker productivity has become a goal for many types of organizations. Increasing productivity refers not only to such matters as a production process but also, for example, making the processing and manipulation of knowledge more effective and efficient. As has been predicted for robotic systems, knowledge-based systems are expected to contribute to an increase in the effectiveness of a manufacturing organization. Robots, once programmed, primarily reduce direct labor costs. However, in many organizations, overhead costs exceed these attributed to direct labor. It is in the reduction of some of these overhead costs that AI technology is expected to make a contribution.

AI systems that improve the internal operations or functions of an organization are another promising application area. It should be recognized, however, that implementation of a knowledge system for internal use can have a pronounced effect on operating procedures of the various entities within an organization. An example is the system developed to order, configure, schedule and track the activity associated with providing telecommunications equipment to customers. This system interacts with sales, various finance and administration groups, manufacturing, and customer service. Significantly, maintenance of the knowledge base and user interface was moved successfully from the computer programmers to the product specialists where it is now processing a thousand engineered systems daily (Whalen and Skoronski, 1986).

The development and use of a knowledge system can help both new and experienced managers to understand the dynamics of their organization's activities. It also assists experienced managers to evaluate the knowledge and assumptions that they use in directing their organizations.

Another benefit which might be obtained with knowledge systems intended to assist humans is the increase in the user's capacity to respond to a greater range of work assignments, thereby improving quality and consistency.

Marketing is another area which will be affected by knowledge systems. Consider how the introduction of other technologic advances have altered traditional marketing methods. For example, the widespread availability of automated bank teller machines has substantially affected the delivery of banking services. A similar effect on distribution channels and sales outlets will result from the incorporation of AI technology into complex products and services. Retail computer stores are using a knowledge system with a minimal AI content to assist customers in selecting from a wide variety of software packages. The interactive system considers the interests and inclinations of both buyer and seller. Increased use of these systems using AI technology will add further impetus to the changing roles of producers, distributors, and customers in this industry.

Knowledge systems can be used, for example, to improve the responsiveness of the development and marketing efforts of a company to shortened product life cycles. Advanced systems include facilities for making educated guesses on competitive reactions. They are also being used to facilitate the selection and implementation of product enhancements which respond to rapidly changing market trends. Indeed, such systems can enable some marketing organizations to lead market trends rather than just respond to them. Many consumer and military products now include a manufacturer's warranty. This can represent a significant cost. Warranty expenses can be reduced by providing service personnel with knowledge systems.

In summary, the widespread introduction of knowledge systems will profoundly affect the way organizations and personnel perform their functions. Similar to the manner in which some of the traditional demarcations between engineering and manufacturing are becoming blurred, procedures and responsibilities for generating and disseminating information will also change. How enterprises deal with customers, suppliers, government, etc., will be impacted. (It may no longer be possible to soothe an irate customer by blaming the computer. The knowledge system may insist on explaining where the problem really is!)

SOME BENCHMARKS

There are a wide range of views presented in the literature about how soon artificial intelligence techniques will have a significant impact on industrial, military and commercial businesses. At one extreme is the viewpoint that artificial intelligence will remain confined to the academic world with the emphasis on replicating various aspects of human intelligence. At the other extreme is the position that artificial intelligence is already revolutionizing the way business gets done. Our opinions place us somewhere in the middle of this discussion. We provide some examples and benchmarks in order to assist the reader in evaluating the timing of the maturation of this technology. Based on the examples in this book, it seems as though artificial intelligence technology is actually moving quite rapidly into commercially viable applications. There is an interesting parallel to the genetic engineering industry. Impressive results in university laboratories triggered a rash of new ventures and claims for instantly building large business entities which would be exceptionally profitable. This was soon followed by disillusionment and increasing government attention to the social implications. Finally, however, genetic engineering is taking its place as an important new industry (Dickson, 1985).

For a second example, much of the early and significant research in artificial intelligence was oriented to medical applications. As yet, however, there are few systems in widespread use (Mishelevich, 1985). Although impressive performance has been demonstrated by a few large diagnostic systems built as research programs, few practicing physicians utilize AI-based systems. This may be due to front-end costs, mistrust of claimed performance, unwillingness to delegate responsibility, liability concerns, impersonal interactions, etc. Perhaps some of these concerns will be mitigated by the changing economics of medical practice.

Establishing commercial viability of an AI-based product can be difficult. It can be influenced by a number of factors including:

1. Appropriate marketing (including distribution and support)

2. Acceptance by the user community of a different way of doing things

3. Better performance or capabilities than present techniques based on a user-oriented product design

4. Validation of performance

5. Acceptable initial and ongoing costs

6. Effective user interface

7. Competitive or peer pressure

8. Status of the supplier

SOCIAL IMPLICATIONS

Robotics may be considered as a mechanism for extending human physical capabilities. Artificial intelligence technology may be considered as a tool for extending human mental capabilities. Just as robotics is having a social impact in the industrial workplace, will the use of artificial intelligence systems have implications for job security and work style of knowledge workers? Will the systems be perceived as a threat to humans (Chace, 1985)? If this perception becomes widespread, AI's successful implementation and utilization will be adversely affected (Gandchi and Gandchi, 1985).

In many organizations, an important role is played by personnel whose jobs do not require much technical background, creativity or, perhaps, do not require possession of an engaging personality. Rather, the contribution of these workers is based on knowing, for example, how the paper work flows, the organizational structure, and where the power is. Consider the individual who knows just the right way to fill out a purchase request. Data is entered in such a manner as to be responsive to the requestor, to the person who is approving the purchase request, and to the supplier. What will be the effect on such an individual of making available an expert system to fill out a purchase request if such a system was introduced? Will that individual's unique value to the organization be diminished? Will the introduction of knowledge systems that threaten an organization's employees be postponed until the employees can be retrained?

Much of the world's goods and services are produced by knowledge workers rather than by industrial processes. With the emergence of artificial intelligence technology, concern has been expressed about reducing the amount of human intellectual labor required to produce these knowledge-based goods and services. This concern has been expressed, not by Luddites, but by thoughtful intellectuals who point out that this technology does indeed have some unique aspects. Again, it is appropriate to consider what has been the impact of computers permeating so many human activities. Certainly, individuals have been adversely affected, and nations as well as industries have changed in many aspects. Yet, there are many people gainfully employed in professions which did not exist before the advent of computers. Artificial intelligence systems offer great promise for relief from human mental drudgery and from mind-numbing processes. They also offer the vision of expanding the horizons and capabilities of individuals who might have been destined for much less challenging and rewarding occupations (Nilsson, 1984; Hayes-Roth, 1984).

There has been considerable recent concern about the minimal growth of productivity in the service industries. It has been estimated that this industry purchases as much as 80 percent of the U.S. production of computers and communications equipment services, and therefore is a natural candidate for the use of AI techniques to support productivity improvements (Anon., 1987).

LEGAL IMPLICATIONS

As noted above, knowledge systems are increasingly being used for diagnosis and for providing advice. In some of these circumstances, the issue of liability arises. Product liability has become contentious and a significant source of increasing concern, not only to consumers, but also to industrial organizations and governments as well. If an AI-based medical system issues a recommendation which, when implemented, causes a significant medical problem to a patient, where should the responsibility be placed? Should it be the company that provided the computer on which a system runs; should it be the person who wrote the software; or should it be the domain expert who provided the knowledge? There are no easy answers for this type of question (Boden, 1985). Total reliance on the knowledge system may be socially unacceptable, as well as technically infeasible.

A company designed and produced a system which was intended to assist pilots with aircraft navigation. The knowledge base contained some erroneous information which had been supplied by a government agency. Reliance on this incorrect information tragically caused the death of a pilot. A court ruled against the company on the grounds that the government-supplied information should have been independently verified.

In order to protect the manufacturers of hardware and software used in air traffic control, the Federal Aviation Administration conducts formal acceptance procedures for all equipment that it purchases. One manufacturer of a system that automatically analyzes a sample from a patient to provide a medical test and provides a printed output containing a recommendation for action has dealt with the problem of liability by including a signature space for the physician owning or operating this equipment to sign the result, thus accepting the responsibility for the recommendation.

As noted in subsequent chapters, the intent of the designers of many knowledge systems is not to replace the human expert; rather it is intended to assist an expert in arriving at a conclusion or making a recommendation. Medical systems typically would aid a physician in searching through a large and complex interrelated set of symptoms and causes. However, such a system should not be presumed to have the physician's intuitive capabilities, knowledge of the particular patient, or perception of subjective factors. Rather, the system's role is to augment the physician's diagnostic skills. As such, the responsibility and liability would remain where it is now.

3

Applications

TYPES OF APPLICATIONS

Although much more experience with development and use will be required before AI becomes as pervasive as other computer technologies, there are already many examples of practical applications. Various companies and organizations have reported useful results from using AI technology based systems in both their internal and external operations (Hewett and Sasson, 1986). The efficiency and effectiveness of such functions as planning, market analysis, electronic design and quality control are being improved by the utilization of AI-based systems. Similarly, AI techniques are being used to provide new features to products and services.

An exhaustive list of AI applications is beyond the scope of this book. For current listings of some of the types of the rapidly growing list of AI applications, the reader is referred to specialized reports and their frequent updates prepared by various market research organizations (Walker and Miller, 1986; Harmon, 1986). The following sections of this chapter are intended to provide a brief overview of the broad range of current applications, arranged by general categories.

MANAGEMENT AND ADMINISTRATION

An increasing number of knowledge systems are being built to assist managers in planning activities, for decision support, and to provide improved access to information stored in various data bases. (There are several mature products to provide existing data base structures with AI front ends, which utilize natural language techniques and various translation protocols.) Strategic planning systems can be used to assist in competitive analysis, technology deployment, and resource allocation. Knowledge systems are now used to augment computer-aided instruction (CAI) systems which would otherwise be limited by rigid structures and apparent insensitivity to individual trainee characteristics. "Intelligent" computer-aided instruction systems can be used to provide a flexible dialog with the student, vary the teaching methodology, recognize types and causes of errors, and provide a useful explanation of their reasoning.

Examples of management support applications:

- Document and archive retrieval
- Equipment configuration design
- Plant safety advisor
- Regulatory compliance advisor
- Office automation techniques
- Capital assets analysis
- Personnel assessment
- Legal advice assistance
- Order entry
- Bid and proposal preparation assistance
- Customer service support
- Site planning
- Product distribution
- Consumer goods marketing

SCIENCE AND ENGINEERING

Some of the earliest applications of AI technology had a scientific or engineering orientation. These applications were used to organize and manipulate the large bodies of information and analysis processes used in mass spectrometry analysis, biological classifications, metallurgy, geology, and mathematics. More recently, there has been great interest in utilizing AI in the design of complex products such as semiconductor circuits, automobiles, and aircraft. A promising area for the future application of AI technology is the development of computer software which continues to be very labor intensive and prone to error. Knowledge systems are being used in specifying software requirements (Harandi and Lubars, 1986) and in system simulation (Neilson, 1986). Conventional computer software simulations are sometimes limited in their ability to deal with missing or ill-defined constraints. AI-based simulators can more readily accommodate situations for which a rigidly defined algorithm is not available. In engineering, computer-aided design (CAD) systems have become valuable in reducing many of the "rote" type of design functions. These systems are being augmented with AI capabilities which help in the front end of the design process—problem analysis, system architecture, and functional design.

Examples of scientific and engineering applications:

- Diffraction analysis
- Optical design
- VLSI chip layout
- Image analysis
- Space station design and mission planning
- Power plant design
- Material selection
- Mechanical, plastic and sheet metal design
- Producibility analysis
- Robot sensing, control, and programming
- Synthesis of chemical compounds

- Molecular structure analysis
- Highway design
- User friendly interfaces to scientific instruments

INDUSTRIAL

In keeping with the current emphasis on increasing productivity, potentially high payoffs for knowledge-system investments are to be found in the industrial environment (Anon., 1986). Some very large investments in "hard" automation have not been as successful in increasing productivity as had originally been expected. Problems have included high cost, lack of flexibility, and integration with existing processes and equipments. Some newly introduced knowledge systems provide increased flexibility and are more capable of responding to the vagaries of manufacturing. However, effective utilization of these systems also entails changes in planning and operations (Taylor, 1986). Of particular interest is the application of knowledge systems to process control to provide interpretation of vast amounts of data (Forbus, 1986) and in the actual control of machines and processes. More widespread use of knowledge systems in process control has been hampered by limitations in realtime capabilities, as is discussed in Chapter 4. However, there has been progress made in such areas as high-speed welding (Bangs, 1986).

Another area of great potential is the applications of AI to robotics and vision systems. Improvements in robotic systems may include:

1. Rudimentary decision making based upon incomplete data—for example, getting around an unanticipated obstacle.

2. Value judgements such as correctly identifying a particular part in a group of different parts. (This area is the focus of intensive academic research but still remains difficult.)

3. Flexible response to situations such as finding a part in an incorrect, but nearby, location.

4. Change execution sequences based on new input.

5. Elementary self-teaching (Drogin, 1986).

Much more R&D will be required to fully realize the potential of these systems. Intelligent robots will need to have access to more knowledge about the physical phenomena with which they interact. Examples are understanding how objects are assembled (or disassembled), spatial reasoning, effects of heating, and material transfers resulting in changes in weight or volume (Sohmolze, 1986).

Examples of industrial applications:

- Production planning and scheduling

- Plant and equipment layout

- Process design advisor

- Flexible process simulation systems

- Machinery maintenance

- Energy management

- Handling of hazardous materials

- Production test planning and control

- Inspection

- Quality control and analysis

- Material handling

- Warehousing

- Emergency response procedures

- Tuning of closed-loop control systems

- Factory job tracking

- Group technology

- Computer-aided manufacturing

- Flexible machining systems

- Inventory management

- Tooling design

- Consumer product labeling

FINANCIAL AND LEGAL

Some important aspects of the financial and legal professions have been changing rapidly, particularly in the recent era of government deregulation. Stock brokers, insurance salesman and financial planners must now deal with a much wider range of products. A stockbroker handles numerous types of securities in addition to stocks and bonds. Similarly, attorneys are faced with increasing complexities and diverse requirements. Also in both of these fields, the customer base has broadened and is less likely to have extensive knowledge and experience. However, with the increasing use of personal computers, more nonprofessionals are choosing to make, or at least analyze, their own financial decisions. Knowledge systems are being developed for various classes of users.

Several sophisticated financial planning systems have been introduced. Incorporating some of the expertise of highly skilled professionals, these systems assist in the analysis of capital investment, new product analysis, and alternative investment strategies. At the other extreme, several personal financial planning packages have become available for personal computers. In the legal field, there are new knowledge systems for areas such as tax law, civil claims, precedence, and environmental regulations. There are also personal computer expert systems to provide assistance in preparing individual tax returns and wills.

Examples of financial and legal systems:

- Letter of credit advice

- Mortgage advice

- Financial forecasting

- Interest "swap" transactions

- Estate planning

- Corporate audit

- Political risk assessment

- Insurance underwriting

- Claim assessment

- Investment portfolio assessment
- Security trader assistance
- International treaty regulations
- Government permit review
- Tort analysis
- Regulatory analysis

DIAGNOSTIC SYSTEMS

Perhaps the most widespread application of AI technology has been in the development of diagnostic systems. These automatic and human-assisted knowledge systems classify specialized parameters or locate problems in a wide variety of practical applications. Some systems are utilized by highly skilled professionals, others by non-experts, and still others are embedded in other products or software systems. An indication of the increasing pervasiveness of these systems is the requirement by a major purchaser of robotics that suppliers must now incorporate diagnostic expert systems in their products.

Increasingly, diagnostic expert systems have been able to demonstrate impressive returns on investment. An early example is a system in use at railroad repair shops which assists maintenance personnel in identifying and solving problems in diesel locomotives (Bonissone, 1983). In a more recent application, the expertise of an experienced engineer was incorporated into a system for troubleshooting commercial cooking equipment. With reference to embedded systems, computer products are being provided with expert systems to identify hardware problems, operational difficulties, and make projections on future potential problems.

Examples of diagnostic systems:

- Fan vibration
- Corrosion analysis
- Network diagnosis
- Pipeline operations

- Telephone cables and switching equipment
- Processing materials
- Automobile faults
- Welding defect analysis
- Commercial air conditioning systems
- Power plant problems
- Life support systems

MILITARY AND SPACE

As has been noted, much of the early support for AI research was provided by military agencies. These agencies are faced with complex strategic and operational problems whose solution may be aided by AI technology. However, many of these applications require computational capability or knowledge structures which continue to be beyond the current state of the art, or at least, beyond the computing power of current military systems. As a result, in spite of large expenditures, there are only a relatively few full-scale knowledge systems which have been delivered to field forces. Some space applications have been more tractable, frequently because a large problem can be divided into more easily handled segments.

Some smaller expert systems are being implemented by the military, particularly for equipment diagnostics. Some notable advances have also been made in the area of planning systems and for training personnel. Less advanced in the development cycle are the guidance of autonomous vehicles, pilot's assistant, and large battle management systems. In space applications, there already are systems for controlling, monitoring and diagnosing various space-borne systems. Also in use are mission planning and cargo allocation systems.

Examples of military and space systems:

- Image analysis
- Document security control
- Space station simulation
- Radar, infrared, sonar tracking

- Electronic warfare

- Combat planning

- Map making

- Target identification

- Weapon allocation

- Intelligence data analysis

- Fuel loading

- Emergency response

- Battle simulation

- Satellite planning

- Telemetry data reduction

- Picture enhancement

MEDICAL

Another early field of AI research was oriented to medical knowledge and its application, particularly diagnosis. There is a vast body of knowledge about diseases, their symptoms, and appropriate treatment. Also, numerous experts are available, usually willing to agree on the meaning of a particular body of evidence and the actions to be taken as a consequence. However, to date, there has been limited utilization of these systems by physicians and hospitals. The reasons for this limited use are believed to relate to the political, economic, and emotional aspects of the medical profession and health care industry. There have been a few success stories, particularly for classification and diagnostic systems (Chandrasekaren and Smith, 1985). For example, automated electrocardiogram interpretation and remote on-line consultive decision-support systems are in limited use. Medical data bases with AI front ends are being accessed more frequently. An early research system is INTERNIST which can evaluate and diagnose the symptoms of almost 500 diseases in the field of internal medicine.

Examples of medical systems:

- Drug adverse interaction
- Chest pain diagnosis
- Pulmonary, neurological, blood, kidney and heart problems
- Chemotherapy treatment
- DNA and RNA analysis
- Blood test analysis
- Layman's interface to medical information
- Psychological analysis and treatment
- Administration of medicine to patients
- Selection of antibotics
- Intensive care monitoring
- Glaucoma treatment
- Medical instruction and training

OTHER APPLICATIONS

A broad range of applications of knowledge systems are being evaluated. These are being developed for use in transportation, agriculture, education, consumer products, geology (an early area of interest), weather forecasting and publishing. Interesting agricultural applications include assisting farmers in planning the planting, monitoring, and marketing of crops. An application of significance in the era of transportation deregulation is the allocation of discount seats on commercial airline flights. Many computer-aided instruction systems are being developed by academia and industry. Publishers are increasingly relying on knowledge systems for graphics preparation and for page layouts. There are many other interesting applications of knowledge systems in these diverse areas and the number of in-use systems is increasing rapidly.

Artificial Intelligence Concepts

TERMINOLOGY

Since the mid-1950s, a number of bright computer scientists, social scientists and others have been attempting to simulate various aspects of human intelligence and behavior on computer systems. Most of this work has been funded by the Department of Defense and the National Science Foundation and the goals of this research have been proof of principle, not the development of applications.

Within the last few years a number of attempts have been made both to use the results of this work for industrial and defense applications and to build hardware and software systems for the commercial marketplace that embody some of the approaches used in the research programs. These attempts have been sufficiently successful that there is now an international industry providing various forms of AI-based technology to industry and the Federal Government with a business volume that is projected to exceed $1 billion. Much of the reporting of this industry by the media has tended to combine the results of the research phase with the potential of the application systems that are now becoming available to give a somewhat optimistic picture of the actual state of affairs. A considerable portion of the initial use of this new commercial technology has been to build skills and demonstrate progress in preparation for the building of operational systems so that there is not yet a large number of completed systems in existence.

Because the term artificial intelligence is somewhat misleading and has been the basis for an incredible number of bad jokes, most workers and product companies in this area have tried to find some other term for their products and systems. Thus terms such as "expert systems" and "knowledge-based systems" have been used to describe specific applications of AI technology. Particularly, the idea of an expert system has been used to describe a software system that is based on the procedural rules used by an expert to evaluate data and reach conclusions about the meaning of the data or the actions that should be taken as a result of these conclusions. The major difference between such systems and previous procedural (decision tree) software is that the operating system for the software, the inference engine, can operate at a complexity level that would be difficult or impossible to handle with predetermined procedure for each data set.

From the viewpoint of most readers of this book, the whole issue of "What is AI?" is probably not very important beyond developing a coherent and defendable point of view associated with the intended use of the technology. Much of the current technology and techniques associated with this field will probably become part of such other disciplines as computer science, philosophy, and human resources management. Similar changes have been true in the past since such common methods as time-sharing and interactive graphics in videogames were first developed as part of AI research programs.

Professor Edward Feigenbaum, while explaining the meaning of AI to a distinguished and perplexed scientific review panel for a Department of Defense AI application development program in the late 1970s commented, "If it works, it isn't AI."

Because AI has been a subject of considerable interest, a number of suppliers and developers of software products have embraced the technology and offer products or demonstrations that "contain AI." It is possible that some of this labeling might be controversial among those who have worked in the field for some time. Since most AI appears as software of some sort, many practitioners of conventional software development can recognize aspects of AI programs that could be accomplished with conventional technology.

An industrial engineer replaced an electromechanical controller on a large machine with an electronic controller which included a CRT display. Upon being told the rudimentary aspects of AI technology, the industrial engineer suddenly exclaimed, "Wow, I've been doing AI all along!"

The replacement of a ladder-logic relay system with logic based on integrated circuits is unlikely to be accepted as an application of artificial intelligence technology. We suggest that wise managers, unless they enjoy tautological discussions, should avoid attempts to define what is or is not artificial intelligence.

At a higher level, there has been some confusion over the relationship between available decision-support systems and knowledge-based expert systems. Computer-based decision-support systems have been in use for many years and have provided valuable assistance to decision makers. A drawback to more widespread use of these decision-support systems is a requirement for well defined algorithms. Professors Turbin and Watkins have provided an interesting comparison of decision support systems and expert systems. An interpretation of this comparison is summarized in Table 4.1. The paper focuses on the conventional definition of an expert system and does not extensively address the intelligent assistant approach to AI.

Recently, expert systems have been used to augment conventional decision-support systems. These combined systems provide a better user interface, more efficient procedures for program development and maintenance, and better presentation of alternatives. Other features include explanation facilities and the highlighting of inconsistencies.

The work on AI has had another effect in the area of social science. The precision required to describe aspects of knowledge and

TABLE 4.1	A Comparison of Expert Systems and Decision-Support Systems	
FEATURES	EXPERT SYSTEM	DECISION-SUPPORT SYSTEM
Primary function	Make available knowledge of an expert	Assist in making decisions
Application	Unique, complex, or ill-defined problems	Structured or repetitive problems
Major focus	Dissemination of expertise	Support decision making
Problem domain	Complex, wide (also limited scope domains)	Narrow
Data representation	Symbolic	Numeric
Information in data base	Procedural and factual	Factual
Human interface	System poses questions	Human poses questions
Reasoning capability	Yes, but limited	No
Explanation capability	Yes	No
Source of recommendations	The system	Human (using system input)

Source: Turban and Watkins, 1985

human behavior for use in computer programs as opposed to oral or written language has caused some changes in approach as the true complexity of human information processing and transfer has become more obvious.

Because it is a new and "hot" field, there has been considerable overstatement of the immediate potential associated with the use of this new technology. As might be expected, this overstatement has been matched with equivalent pessimism and there is now considerable debunking literature.

FEATURES

From a management perspective, the greatest interest in artificial intelligence may be its potential for extending human mental capability. The technology is already being used to augment the reasoning ability of humans. Again, this is not meant to imply replacement of the human mind, but rather expansion of its grasp. The reasoning prowess of a knowledge system is rudimentary as compared to a human, but nevertheless, it can provide useful assistance to the human. Such systems also facilitate the acquisition and use of new knowledge and provide guides to the incorporation of incomplete or rapidly changing knowledge. Technologic progress is also being made in improving the support for a reasoning process. Reasoning by example shows great promise as a method. In some cases, the results of the reasoning process may be made available to an intended user in a more effective form than that provided by a human expert.

Frequently, the most prominent characteristic of a business environment is an aura of uncertainty. Decisions must be made based upon incomplete or uncertain data. The implications of the decisions are often difficult to fully comprehend in advance. Computer-based systems have been effectively used to model a business environment. However, in many of these systems it is cumbersome or difficult to model the uncertainties of the business environment. It then becomes necessary to force-fit the "real world" into the structure of the model; rather than being able to structure the model to accurately reflect the business environment. These conventional systems also have problems in dealing with subjective terms such as high, low, fast, slow, warmer, stronger and larger. AI-based techniques are being developed to operate on these subjective terms.

Fuzzy logic deals with computing using the symbolic meaning of words rather than numeric values. If you were asked to explain a common situation such as how to ride a bicycle, your response would undoubtedly be in words and subjective feelings rather than well-defined algorithms. The intent of fuzzy logic is to convert the symbols and words we use to represent feelings and relationships into numeric equivalents which can be manipulated by computational techniques.

An obvious application for AI technology is in the field of robotics. Clearly, the ability to sense the environment in which a robotic system must operate is a critical function. Otherwise, it is necessary to preposition all elements of a task or function to be performed completely and to provide the necessary tool position accuracy at the location of the effector of a robotic system where the actual task will be performed. Robots with six to nine degrees of freedom tend to have an error budget inconsistent with effector positioning for anything but the crudest of task (spray painting, for instance). Obviously, vision sensors, in some form, are a highly attractive approach for going beyond the totally predetermined system operating concept.

There has been much research on vision systems for robotics and inspection applications. In some cases, notably the autonomous land vehicle program, visual-sensing research has become the prime focus of development work. The most success has come in constrained inspection situations, where the detection of significant abnormalities or matching to a constant pattern is the objective. Ultrasonic sonar systems, many using Polaroid™ sensors, have been useful in obstacle avoidance and protecting personnel.

Vision applications are data- and computation-intensive so that realtime operation, even in constrained conditions, can require the use of computing resources that are not consistent with the economics of the situation. Much of the research has focused on the use of a single segmentation or area selection method operating instantaneously on the visual field of interest that attempts to group and then recognize the elements of the scene that is viewed. An example might be the picking of parts from a bin of mixed parts including: recognizing a pickable part, determining the correct orientation of the picking mechanism relative to the part for effective grasping, positioning the picker in grasping position, recognizing the type of part to be picked and accurate placement of the picked part at its final destination.

It is reasonable to assume that dual cameras can give at least limited three-dimensional (3D) information, although even calculated 3D positions can be inaccurate if the location of highlights or appearance of a part is sensitive to the look angle. If the parts to be described have complex surfaces, as would be true in any nontrivial picking operation, the problem becomes one of bounding a large search space, difficult to describe in advance, which contains all the possible patterns that would be seen from any part, in any location, in any orientation.

Research is underway on various aspects of this area including various scene segmentation algorithms that group areas on the basis of similarity in texture, intensity or location. Other research is devoted to probabilistic recognition methods where decisions are made on the basis of best fit to a goal using a number of independent measures.

Human visual recognition is probably a language-like process where primitive operators, like phonemes, are combined into more complex concepts, like words, and integrated over time and experience into more complex concepts, like sentences, paragraphs and chapters. The analogy is anything but exact; however, if the complexity of the recognition problem becomes clear in terms of the power of human visual processing compared to current hardware processing speeds and software capability, our point has been made. We suspect that truly effective vision processing systems will probably emerge when parallel processing systems are available with total implementation costs that match the current hardware development potential of very large scale integration (VLSI).

In some areas, the proliferation of knowledge has been so great that even the highly competent experts cannot be aware of all the implications of using this knowledge. An example is the increasing number of drugs and treatments available to modern medicine. It is difficult for the medical professional to have complete knowledge of possible drug interactions. Systems are being introduced, even at the local pharmacy, which are capable of pointing out potential drug interaction problems. Knowledge systems augment these capabilities by interacting with either the physician or the patient to uncover additional potential problems. These systems, incidentally, can also be of assistance in responding to the demands and liabilities of medical practice (Gayle and Dankel, 1986).

Other valuable components of AI technology that we believe will come into more general use are the various AI programming tools that have been developed to assist a programmer or system designer to understand the logic and control structure of a program. These tools were developed out of necessity to help an AI system programmer understand and debug the complex structures that were developed, particularly in the rapid prototyping mode that has characterized much of AI system research and development. As computational power and high resolution graphics become available at low cost, it will be appropriate to provide powerful development and maintenance tools to support the most mundane programming tasks. Using such technology, detailed descriptions and graphic animations can be presented which indicate relationships, programming techniques and reasoning processes that have been used.

Horror stories abound relating the difficulty of maintaining a software package when the original software designer is no longer available. It is difficult to understand the original designer's thought processes and, even with the best of documentation, it is often hard to comprehend the relationships between various elements of the program. AI-based programs offer a promise of providing much better indication of the structure of the software program as well as facilitating modifications and updates.

In one laboratory, a programmer had been developing a package using AI techniques. He had left a computer print- out of his code sitting on the table. A second programmer, who had no previous contact with the project, happened by and looked at the computer printout. The AI techniques used to implement and document the software code made it easy for the second programmer to understand the program. Curiosity led to further reading and inadvertent discovery of a bug in the program. It was easy to convince the original programmer that there indeed was a bug in the program. Both were impressed with how much easier it would be to maintain this type of software.

LIMITATIONS

Although the features noted in the previous section are valuable, it is necessary to be aware of limitations of AI-based technology. Some of these limitations are being removed with the rapid advance of technology. As depicted in Figure 4.1, other limi- tations are of a more fundamental nature, particularly in duplicat- ing basic human capabilities. These include such human traits as in- tuition, learning, and sensory perceptions (taste, vision, smell and touch) (Dreyfus and Dreyfus, 1986). Another difficult problem is the development of systems that reason from basic principles and evalu- ate the relative value of multiple opinions.

Interesting research is being conducted on machines which mimic the human brain's interconnected neurons. In their present state, these machines exhibit a rudimentary ability in reading, speech and vision (Anon., 1986; Port, 1986).

Other research with rudimentary neural networks has dem- onstrated random passing of information between neurons in the net. One system uses a "reward" mechanism to eventually select the best path along the network. Potential applications include robot controllers and seeking paths around obstacles (Handle and Hastings, 1986).

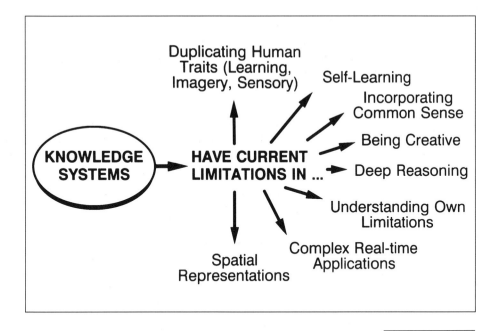

Figure 4.1
Current Limitations of Knowledge Systems

Perhaps one of the greatest limitations of knowledge systems is the difficulty of incorporating common sense or intuition. Even a child realizes that one does not move a glass full of milk by first turning it upside down. Yet, for sophisticated AI systems, many detailed common sense reactions must somehow be laboriously incorporated into the system design. Even then it is difficult for the designers to perceive all the possible situations in which ordinary common sense would apply.

It seems likely that the term "common sense" contains several important and difficult-to-implement concepts. One concept is that of private knowledge that is discussed, at length, in Chapter 7. We believe that private knowledge, to a much greater extent than the current literature would indicate, is capturable and usable based on the application of the approach of that chapter.

A second concept is the recognition of context and the ability to recognize the applicability of specific knowledge in that context.

Using the example of the glass of milk given above, the common-sense rule would not necessarily apply if the milk was frozen or if it had a tight lid. This topic is discussed at greater length later in this chapter in the section on Control.

Finally, there is the capability for causal reasoning based on experience and knowledge. This topic is the subject of research as a form of naive physics. "Milk is a fluid, fluids spill or seek the lowest level in a gravity field and a glass is a hollow object, designed to hold fluids in a certain orientation. . ."(DeKleer and Seeley-Brown, 1984).

The difficulty in incorporating common sense into a knowledge system is a good reason for not endeavoring to replace totally the human expert in many applications. In addition to humans usually having common sense, they are also more capable of adapting to unanticipated situations; they can be more creative; be more sensitive to subjective factors; and they are likely to be more aware of peripheral issues. Another important human trait is the ability to rank objects on a numeric scale of values. Typically, this action employs some sort of subjective reasoning. Examples are: providing a numerical score to Olympic diving events and a movie critic's assignment of a number of stars to a movie one likes or dislikes. Note that these rankings are not really a probability which can be mathematically manipulated. The rankings involve individual levels of perception, and it is difficult to put this type of perceptive attitude into a knowledge system.

Much AI research has been devoted to methodologies for assigning certainty factors or probabilities, but these methodologies are different than the subjective ranking capability humans frequently use.

Another limitation of many knowledge systems is the distinction between shallow and deep reasoning. In a diagnosis system, rules can be implemented which direct the technician to read a voltage at a particular point on a circuit board. If the voltage is outside of stated limits, the board should be replaced. Contrast this shallow reasoning system with one that could incorporate the laws of physics governing the movement of electrons in semiconductors. If such deep reasoning could be incorporated in the system, it would be more capable of responding to situations which had not been anticipated.

In addition to being constrained by shallow reasoning, knowledge systems generally lack a capability for internal reflection. In arriving at a recommendation, did the system appropriately consider other possible solutions, or did it just use an arbitrary process of elimination? Or, what are the implications of the information the system is asking the user to provide? Is this information expensive or difficult to obtain, not really important or pertinent, etc.? Designers of some diagnostics systems are attempting to compensate for this inadequacy (Lenat, 1983). Before asking the user for additional data, the system will take into account how expensive it would be to run additional tests and the potential value of the information that would be obtained from the results.

If developable, deep reasoning systems would be of value to managers faced with making broad-ranging policy decisions.

Another important but difficult problem is the ability of a system to "learn." Clearly, this is an important component of human capability shared to a greater or lesser extent by all living organisms. There has been some ambitious academic research on this topic, whose immediate practical value is uncertain.

It seems unlikely that human-level learning systems are in the immediate future. More realistic in the near term is the teachable system (Lenat, 1983; Lenat, n.d.; Ritchie and Hanna, 1984). In fact, teachable systems are even offered without reference to AI in the PC environment. An interface to a relational data base can be designed by laying out a form, or a spreadsheet equivalent can be built by writing formulas rather than programming operations in spreadsheet language. The teachable AI system will probably be based on the combination of a high-level design language for the user plus tools that will show the results in both logical operations and flow of control that result from user changes in the system.

Further away, but still possible, are systems that, to some extent, can evaluate the results of change and point to probable consequences.

A major difficulty in implementing learning systems is due to the limitation of our knowledge about how humans learn and how to reproduce this process in software to any extent. Other limitations are due to the lack of the type of sensory input for AI systems that are similar to those that humans use to acquire much of their knowledge. Humans can learn how to do something by watching others do it. For example, an apprentice can more readily understand how to assemble a complex mechanism if the printed instructions are supplemented by a physical demonstration. A comparable learning process is difficult to reproduce in a knowledge system. This lack of learning capability not only limits the system's performance but also increases the possibility of obsolescence as the knowledge base changes.

Another inherent problem is the system's unawareness of the limitations on its own knowledge. Without careful design, many knowledge systems do not fail gracefully. When confronted with a situation for which they really do not have adequate knowledge or reasoning mechanism, the systems may not indicate an inability to respond. Rather, they may derive a grossly incorrect or irrelevant conclusion. Sometimes the difficulty is caused by a minor aberration such as receiving input which is phrased slightly differently from what was expected. A response on a CRT that insists the user has made an input error by providing a misphrased, but otherwise correct, element of input heightens the irritation since the human perceives very little difference between the two elements of input.

Realtime applications have been a difficult problem for builders of knowledge systems. Knowledge systems can usually provide information to human operators at an acceptable rate, but not fast enough or reliably enough for such applications as process control. One problem is simply computational complexity. These programs have a large search space to explore and require considerable computational power to do so in realtime. A second problem is overhead operations. The LISP language creates memory allocations for each operation and an overhead function called garbage collection must be performed periodically to reclaim memory that is no longer needed. A third problem is truth maintenance. As each new fact or data point is processed, it is possible that previous results are no longer valid. The knowledge system searches through its knowledge base, using criteria and input data to arrive at preliminary conclusions which are subsequently built upon. However, if the knowledge system assumes that "time stands still" during the search period, some of the premises which were initially found to be true may be no longer be valid because the input data has already changed.

For early AI programs, where batch processing of a fixed data set was done, this was not a problem. However, for realtime data, truth maintenance can be computationally impossible. The knowledge system must sort through realtime input and ascertain what is relevant, true, contradictory, etc. This information can be skewed by system noise which is inadvertant or, even worse, intentionally inaccurate. As each data point is received, the system must also check that previous tentative or firm conclusions are still valid in the light of the new data. All of these topics are the subject of continuing and active research and considerable progress has been made. However, the manager must recognize that the true magnitude of the realtime problem may not become clear during the evaluation of a limited-scale prototype. A reserve of 20–30 percent of total development time should be saved at the end of the expected development cycle for tuning to increase processing speed to an acceptable level.

Another problem in realtime application is the combinatorial growth of alternative solutions caused by rapidly changing input. Dealing with this combinatorial growth places great strain on the available computing resources (processing time constraints, costs, physical limitations). An approach to coping with this combinatorial growth is to endeavor to select intelligently those hypotheses most likely to lead to an acceptable answer. This may be augmented by the use of approximation (Green, 1986). Since the potential market is large, there is much R&D on hardware and software intended for operation in realtime systems. Some successes have been reported in such areas as process control and military systems.

Another challenging area of research is sensors and sensor processing for robotic systems. One school of thought, primarily Japanese, recognizes the limitations of current technology and adapts component design and manufacturing methods to what is currently available. The implementation strategy focuses on robots with limited degrees of freedom, prepositioned parts and component design that facilitates robot assembly. American research has focused more on flexible mechanical "people" with heavy demands on sensors, sensor processing and robotic operations programming. As any investor in high-technology robotics well knows, results have not quite lived up to expectations.

Still another limitation relates to human interaction with a knowledge system. Great progress has been made, but there are still many applications where entering or manipulating information is awkward. An example is engineering design where physical objects frequently must be operated upon in terms of fundamental geometric shapes, rather than with the use of well-accepted engineering or manufacturing terminology. Rather than describing an object as, say, a combination of cylinders and pyramids, it would conceptually be much easier to work with flanges, rims and hubs. Not only would such terms be easier to understand but the properties of an object on the basis of its particular conceptual meaning could be attached to each object. (A flange implies gaskets, bolt holes and bolts, for example.) To match the capability described above, users of current systems are required to perform extensive subdivision of their work. New techniques are being developed that will be more capable and have increased performance in the recognition of shape. Perhaps these techniques will provide a basis for increased automation of this part of design activity. Certainly, using humans for generation of symbolic meaning for shapes in drawings could also provide the input data for expert systems with detailed design knowledge.

The above catalog of limitations does appear formidable. But consider the available alternatives—how effective or trustworthy are they? A medical diagnosis system may be shallow in its reasoning structure and limited in its common sense reaction to patient input. Yet, even with these deficiencies, it would have great social value by making available medical advice in remote parts of the world.

TECHNOLOGY

Languages

One of the first steps in the development of AI in the universities was the writing of a new language, LISP, which has become one of the central features of AI and is almost as old as FORTRAN in its history of use. LISP is an acronym for List Processing Language and includes many capabilities that support the requirements of a symbolic and logical process generation. Until recently, most of the AI research in the United States was done in LISP, although every self-respecting research institution had its own dialect or version of the language. Because of the power available to the programmer, LISP programs tend to make heavy use of available processing power in a conventional computer. It has proved cost-effective to build several generations of single user super-minicomputers with architecture specialized for LISP processing.

Recently, the Department of Defense (DOD) recognized the need for more commonality in the research and development activity that it has been funding. Using fairly strong pressure on its contractors, DOD has sponsored the development of Common LISP as a language of choice for future research and development. The major problem with this approach is that some of the more useful features of the LISP environment are yet to be specified in Common LISP (Steele, 1984).

During the 1970s workers at the University of Marseilles developed a language, PROLOG, that was designed to support logical operations and provide the operating system to control the processing of logical analysis (Colmerauer *et al.*, 1981). This language has been extensively used for research and application development in Europe and Asia and is gaining some acceptance in the United States. Part of the reason for the use of PROLOG is that it is less demanding of mainframe computer resources and certain types of expert systems. More specifically, data-base analysis can be written directly and easily in this language. Beyond these two languages, there are several other higher-level languages that include various forms of procedure control such as OPS-5 (Hayes-Roth *et al.*, 1983).

Development environments

Given that a hundred or so primitive computer operations have been implemented in hardware or efficient machine code, it is possible to write the entire operating system of a computer in LISP as well as the higher level software for an AI system. Further, a network of such computers can be created and hosted on a mainframe of reasonable size. Methods for fast and efficient file maintenance and transfer and electronic mail within a network also exist. Recently, it has been found possible to write efficient compilers for more conventional code in LISP so that it is possible to integrate or develop more conventional language programs in a LISP development environment as well. This flexibility, as well as the availability of powerful diagnostic processes, developed over the years in the academic community, makes it possible to provide a group of skilled programmers an individually customized, but joint, software development environment. This environment contains many tools and processes that can be adapted to provide many of the process components of software that are expensive and tedious to write in conventional code. Experience with these development environments has shown significant increases in speed (2 to 3 times), for the development of both small and large prototype systems over that expected with more conventional technology (Waterman, 1986).

In evaluating the purchase or use of a specific version of an AI language, the power and capability of the associated development environment should be given major importance. In fact, for the development of complex systems, the productivity gains mentioned above can only be obtained with a powerful development environment. It is possible that the strength of the market for high-end LISP machines is primarily a factor of the development environments that come with them rather than the specific power of the hardware or the basic language facility that they provide. In general, available LISP development environments are more complete than for other languages probably because the language has been used both longer and by more AI research groups. Initial steps toward development of PROLOG development environments have been made in Japan (Anon., 1984–1985).

Another part of the AI development environment philosophy has been the concept of the open system. There is an implicit assumption that users of this development environment will be both skilled and responsible individuals. Some protection is provided by individual file and buffer saving and protection methods but the kind of protection against incompetent, malicious, or criminal activity found in conventional mainframe operating systems does not exist in these environments. This open philosophy is not necessarily a disadvantage under many conditions but is unlikely to be acceptable, without modification, under most conditions of operational use. If nothing else, the unskilled user who makes an error and is provided with complex diagnostic information and powerful control logic intended to help a skilled programmer find a bug, is unlikely to know what to do. The creation of a relatively bombproof interface for the naive but properly motivated user for a system with complex, menu-driven interaction capability operating in a development environment, involves from 6 to 12 additional person-months of effort after the user interface design has stabilized.

We are not aware of any development environment that has adequate protection against malicious or criminal use.

Another factor to be considered in the use of these environments is their stability. Most machine suppliers have emphasized the sophisticated programmer as a target market; thus there is strong pressure to provide this market with the latest and best in software technology. Under these conditions, the stability of the operating system and other features that are utilized in existing code can sometimes suffer as new releases appear. Since maintaining multiple releases is not supported or encouraged by either disk storage requirements or manufacturer maintenance policies, program maintenance across releases can sometimes require considerable effort in these environments.

Processes and data structures

The terms "processes and data structures" are used here to describe components of an AI system such as an inference engine or a data-base structure. At the present time, there has been little commercial development of specific AI system components, although it seems possible that such capabilities may become available in the near future. However, there is a rich literature on AI methodology derived from the academic community and examples of many different approaches can be found in it (Barr and Feigenbaum, 1981).

One of the problems that has been solved to a considerable extent is the definition of data structures that are appropriate for the representation of various forms of knowledge. The development of a system that uses human knowledge is much easier if the representation structure in which this knowledge is imbedded matches the general form or context from which this knowledge is derived or based. For example, some types of knowledge are "frame oriented."

Frame-oriented knowledge tends to have a number of associated items with each major category; so that a house will have windows, doors, walls, etc. Where time is a significant factor, a script-oriented representation is often used. Going to a restaurant is often used as an example because there are normally common elements in time sequence involved with eating a meal in a restaurant like ordering from a menu, getting a check and paying the bill.

One process frequently used is the blackboard architecture. This concept was first used for research on speech recognition on the HEARSAY project. The idea is implementation of a multiprocessing model where a series of interrelated processes are built that communicate by passing messages to each other. This arrangement simplifies the job of controlling such processes, since their interaction is at a relatively simple level and the complexity of the control problem for the system is considerably reduced.

Representation methods

Representation methods are the heart of an AI system. Such methods are used to contain the knowledge in an expert system and to provide a mechanism for a control structure for the system. There are many excellent texts available that describe these methods in multiple levels of detail (Winston, 1984; Charniak and McDermott, 1984). The remainder of this section is intended to provide a minimal introduction to the topic, not to supplement these texts.

There has been a continuing effort to use the methods of formal logic to represent reasoning processes. Unfortunately, human reasoning sometimes does not follow formal paths and there are now continuing and heated arguments of the general nature that "birds fly"—that is, unless they are dead or ostriches, etc. The neophyte will hear continued reference to "non-monotonic reasoning" which tends to mean that something is true unless it is not.

A large body of expert systems are written as production rules of the form: *if* a certain condition is satisfied, *then* take a specific action. It should be noted that knowledge and action or control are mixed in a production-rule system. Thus, when a new piece of information becomes available to a production-rule system, the inference engine must decide the order in which multiple rules that are satisfied simultaneously are processed and prevent unwanted behavior. Control logic remains a difficult issue in the design and maintenance of large production-rule systems.

There are several schemes used to store knowledge in a form believed to be similar to that used by humans. A frame stores information that is pertinent to a central concept which is the subject of the frame and may include pointers of various sorts to other frames that store additional pertinent information. A frame may also include control procedures that are pertinent to the concept. Semantic nets describe relationships between nodes or objects. Scripts or scenarios permit the inclusion of time relationships between objects.

Explanation systems

One of the widely advertised features of an expert system is the ability to explain the chain of reasoning that led to a particular conclusion. In general, these explanation systems are based on "inferencing" systems that keep track of the specific rules that have "fired" or have their input conditions satisfied. Where this is possible, the explanation consists of the text of the rules that have fired with the input values that caused the firing. The specific order of firing, when several rules have their input conditions satisfied, is determined by the control logic in the inference engine. It should be noted that this level of explanation is not necessarily equivalent to human logic patterns nor are structured, semi-English rules particularly readable. It is possible that effective explanation systems may require an intermediate expert system that converts what is essentially diagnostic information for the system developer into a lucid and understandable explanation.

An expert system was designed to provide diagnostic information about a manufacturing process. The showing of the text of rules that had fired had little value to the operators who tested the system. It was necessary to design a separate explanation system based on causal reasoning that explained the logic of the system in meaningful terms.

A word of caution is in order. Psychological experiments have indicated that individuals are inclined to accept, without their usual degree of analysis, what appears to be a plausible reason if it is generated by a computer.

SEARCH

Another significant requirement is the need to find an efficient method for reducing the amount of computational searching for a match or a solution. Considerable important work has been done on the problem of pruning a search space without affecting the result of the search. One technique is to compare the value of completing a particular branch versus another. Of course, the measurement of value is a problem. As realtime applications become more important, search methods must become even more efficient in order for an AI system to run in real-time.

NATURAL LANGUAGE UNDERSTANDING

There has been an increasing amount of work on the problem of language understanding. Early work was focused on direct pattern matching in speech recognition and parsing sentences in processing written language. More recently, there has been more use of knowledge about the structure of language and speech to reduce the computational requirements and improve the accuracy of the results. There are several systems that can recognize as many as several thousand words, enough for a fairly extensive command set in a "hands busy" application but not enough for business text entry (dictation to text).

A number of production natural language command systems are capable of understanding structured English commands. These systems are context-sensitive and require that a situation-specific grammar and vocabulary be created for each application.

AUTOMATIC PROGRAMMING

An obvious application for AI technology is in the development of software without some of the more tedious aspects of coding. There has been some research on various aspects of software program development. Arthur D. Little, Inc. has developed a structured English to LISP compilation system for a client and an equivalent commercial system has recently been announced.

It should soon be possible to build a Programmer's Assistant that will assist in the more routine aspects of code development although no development has apparently been completed beyond a system that assists in the training of ADA programmers (C* Thought) and a prototype system that converts a logical diagram to LISP (Reasoning Systems). True automatic programming that will relieve a programmer of the responsibility for logical design seems to be some time in the future.

REASONING AND PROBLEM SOLVING

The higher-level aspect of human intelligence like the ability to reason and solve problems have been attractive topics for research since the beginning of work in this field. Although there have been a number of secondary benefits from this research in the form of representation methods and other technologies, success in this field has been elusive. Some efforts have been along the lines of positioning millions of monkeys sitting at typewriters but the problem of finding something "interesting" in random noise has been difficult. One "learning" system that appeared to find "interesting" mathematical relationships did not stand up well to critical external review (Lenat and Brown, 1984; Ritchie and Hanna, 1984).

CONTROL

The typical AI system consists of data or information, rules that operate or act on this information and a control mechanism to make the whole thing perform its required job. Many expert system shells and some high-order languages come with a built-in control mechanism called an inference engine. Providing effective control is one of the most difficult aspects of AI system design and one of the barriers to "intelligent behavior." If one looks at how human expertise operates, it might be said that true human intelligence consists of islands of linearity surrounded by large swamps of nonlinearity. Each linear island is context-dependent and within a pertinent context, can probably be the subject of a rule-based description. Except in certain well-bounded situations, the rules are not necessarily invariant across islands and may not apply at all in the nonlinear areas.

In a rule-based system, the control mechanism must select the appropriate order for rules to fire and select those that are appropriate. This is not a trivial task and to a considerable extent becomes a situation-specific art. The problem is particularly acute at the edges of the islands and in the swamps. Basically, the control system must recognize that some rules do not apply in certain situations and adapt its control strategy to each situation.

Another problem is the fact that rule firing is normally a string-matching or pattern recognition method. Each rule does not recognize meaning but only identity. Thus, just because a medical diagnosis system has been told that a patient is overweight, it would not also know that there was a very high probability that the patient was also fat, and might ask additional questions that were already implicitly answered by the response to the question about overweight. In order to prevent this problem, the designer of the system must include rules in the knowledge base that recognize these relationships. Providing the appearance of understanding in an interactive computer program can be a difficult job because of the need to match the richness of conceptual understanding in the human. It is likely that most operational interactive systems are continually "patched" on the basis of experience until the system has enough "knowledge" about the meaning of its data base for it not to appear stupid to the user. The use of menu-based interaction as opposed to conversational interaction may save the builder a lot of work during the initial introduction of an operational system.

At the research level, there is a continuing struggle to deal with the problems of non-monotonic reasoning. The problem is that a fact or rule is only sometimes true. An elaborate empirical and context-sensitive control system may be needed to deal with reasoning systems that work under conditions that depend on non-monotonic logic. Another topic requiring additional research is the use of probability in a logical system. At the present time there is no general system for using probability in connection with a rule base. There is usually so much context dependence in an uncertain situation that probability estimates for the combination of several rules have little actual meaning.

NETWORKS

An important component of the current methods of building large AI software systems on high-end LISP machines is the use of networks hosted on a file server. Part of the development environment available on these machines is support for file transfer and electronic mail between systems and a control system for revisions of commonly used software routines. Such a network permits a group of programmers to work closely and rapidly to build and debug a complex software system. One important factor is the self-documenting features of the LISP language that permit a group of programmers to understand and mutually interface with reasonably annotated code. The electronic mail system can be used for higher-level reports on progress and problems that have been encountered and fixed.

In addition to the development environment, various forms of distributed AI applications are coming into use. In one form, cooperating expert systems are networked with some commonality of knowledge bases. This is a useful method of reducing the maintenance problems associated with a large rule-based system. If a large system can be broken down into individual modularized elements, the interactions between systems are at a higher level and easier to visualize and control. (Here is another example of re-learning the lessons that the non-AI programming community has learned from several decades of experience.)

Another approach being used increasingly is the imbedded AI subsystem. Several mainframe manufacturers and niche firms are offering shells that support the imbedding of small AI systems in a larger conventional application. As VLSI technology is successfully applied to the building of AI systems and subsystems, it seems probable that imbedding or hosting AI subsystems supported on special purpose boards will be possible. The details of interfacing these boards with the host computer will be provided by the supplier, so an AI subsystem, developed by "rapid prototyping" technology, can be downloaded into a board with little or no effort.

PRODUCTIVITY VERSUS CAPITAL COSTS

There are some significant cost trade-offs issues that require evaluation, associated with the hardware and software environment that is made available to AI system developers. In selecting an environment, the available range extends from a $100 software package that runs on a PC to a high-end development machine and a general-purpose shell that might cost $200,000 exclusive of training cost. At the low end, there appear to be a number of areas where even the most elementary form of AI system can have a real effect on productivity. In these environments, a low-cost solution can provide immediate and visible improvement and thus provide justification for more advanced AI system development capability. With more complex requirements, a simple environment may only be a source of frustration for those trying to use it. We believe that for a simple system, the chances of success are higher if the expert and the AI system developer are the same person. The motivation for successful use is higher and the expert is likely to recognize, immediately, both problems with the system and methods, not necessarily using either AI technology or computers, to compensate for them.

An expert assistant system was carefully built to support a renowned expert in his daily work. The system had a dramatic impact on the productivity of the expert, reducing the time for execution of certain routine tasks from weeks to hours. However, when the system was transferred to more general use by less qualified experts, problems arose, because the less qualified experts did not recognize that the system was giving wrong answers when used under inappropriate conditions.

It is important for the manager to understand the current level of uncertainty about the applicability of any particular technology because of general lack of experience with specific applications. "Show me successful and directly related examples" is a wise request when considering the purchase of the current versions of the more expensive hardware and software technology. Some early pioneers went the high-end route and found themselves with a capability that was unneeded; others tried the low-end route and were only able to develop toy applications. Equivalent experience can be a valuable commodity in making this trade-off whether it is hired, or obtained from vendors, academics or consultants.

"RAPID PROTOTYPING"

Builders of software systems have always used whatever quick methods were available to construct a version of a software system for evaluation by designers and users during the early stages of system development. This approach is usually called "Rapid Prototyping." However, the speed with which a relatively high level of system capability can be reached is probably specific to the use of AI technology. It should be understood, however, that a rapid prototype built with AI technology is in no way an operational system in the conventional sense. The complexity that can be developed with extensive use of AI technology can be both expensive to convert and maintain with more conventional operational methods. Thus it is important for a manager to recognize the true life cycle cost of a complex AI system that currently only exists as a prototype. The eventual user and the source of funds for system development and maintenance must be educated on the potential cost before launching into the operational development phase.

It should be recognized that a rapid prototype can be used as a way to develop a user-evaluated functional specification that can later be converted into a conventional system without as many of the adjustment and maintenance problems as might be encountered with a system built with more conventional specification methods.

NATURE OF THE POSSIBLE

The reader of this book will probably notice that the potential impact of AI technology is sometimes presented with great enthusiasm and sometimes with considerable caution. Some of this schizophrenia is due to the different outlooks of the two authors who tend to regard the world from opposite ends of the enthusiasm-pessimism spectrum. Beyond personal viewpoints however, is the uncertainty associated with any new technology. Both authors agree that AI technology will undoubtedly revolutionize the productivity of many components of American and world industry as AI comes into more general use. On the other hand, it is not necessarily true that introduction of this technology will be either easy or cheap. After all, software is software, whether AI or not, and all the problems associated with the development and maintenance of complex software still remain.

Rapid prototyping technology and knowledge engineering methods can be used to improve the specification process for large and complex systems, whether AI technology-based or not. Also, many well-bounded areas of human decision making should benefit from the use of rule-based systems. If the decision space for a system is not well bounded, it is more likely that an intelligent assistant system will be appropriate. Going beyond these limits to the areas of human capability in decision-making under uncertainty or learning from experience seems unlikely in the near future. Such capability in a computer will probably not be feasible except in limited demonstrations until both the hardware and software for massively parallel computing are commercially mature.

THE DELIVERY ENVIRONMENT

Since much of the work on AI applications was until recently an investigation of the potential of the technology and serious application development was still in progress, less attention by both suppliers and users has been given to delivery systems. This lack of attention is likely to cause and perhaps may have already slowed the further growth of the field. For many, a delivery system was the equivalent of a low-cost machine, without a powerful LISP development environment, that could be used to run the code written on a development machine. Since most prototypes were deliberately designed to avoid the cost of integration, the possible scale, cost and risk of this part of the software development cycle were not obvious. More recent experience has shown that this part of the process is not without risk and may cost as much as the prototype itself (Davis, 1981). Thus, the large group of potential, but as yet uncommitted, industrial users whose commitment to the use of AI technology has been assumed by the forecasters of the future market for this technology, may actually be waiting for evidence that the true cost and risk of a working installation is both known and acceptable.

High-end machine producers are giving belated attention to workable interfaces with large mainframes for their equipment and to consider low-end, lower-cost machines without development capability. High-end shell makers have been rewriting their products in languages that are used on non-AI machines. At least one supplier of a shell has announced a product that interfaces with a large mainframe data-base product. As mentioned earlier, there are a number of shells and versions of AI languages like LISP and PROLOG that run on PC-level machines. It is expected that RSIC and 32-bit word PCs will bridge the performance gap between the PC and the high-end machines.

A robust technology for translation from a rapid prototype to a stable operational system and for routine maintenance and enhancement of that system, however, still remains to be developed. There will probably be a range of delivery systems with different stability requirements depending on the flexibility for change that is needed. If the system needs to be changed frequently, its maintenance will be done by methods closer to rapid prototyping and more attention given to user-friendly error-recovery techniques. If the system is stable, it will probably be written and maintained with present-day conventional methods. A further discussion of delivery systems is presented in Chapter 13.

It has been tempting for some users to carry out system development on a delivery system. The flexibility and power of the development environment may be significantly less but the transition problems from development to operational use are obviously reduced. As potential delivery systems become more powerful, this alternative becomes even more attractive. Minimizing the risk and cost of development software transition to operational status should have high priority in the high-end machine and shell market. The recent slump in the market for such systems may have something to do with lack of attention to this issue and that it will receive much more focused level of attention in the very near future from those suppliers affected by the slump.

STATUS

For a long time, AI was of interest primarily to researchers. Although this research has been going on for many years, AI must still be considered a new field. Perhaps two-thirds of the people developing deliverable knowledge systems have been in the field for less than five years. Advances in theory, hardware and software are now providing the impetus to use AI technology in many different types of applications. Substantial investments are being made by both small and large organizations as well as government and other institutions. These investments have been made over a fairly wide range. Some companies have established large groups that carry out both AI R&D with an academic flavor and provide training to disciples who then go out and diffuse the technology in their own divisions. Other companies, as with the infusion of PC technology, are introducing AI on almost an ad hoc basis, usually using the low-end PC-based systems as a way of providing motivated individuals with a way to use the technology at low capital cost. By 1987, one company was planning to build and use about 2,000 knowledge systems over the succeeding five years. The company predicted corporate earnings increases of 10 percent due to the use of these knowledge systems (Williamson, 1987).

There are also many start-up companies. There have been at least 50 new venture capital companies in the last five years.

Recently, AI has been "blessed and given the stamp of legitimacy" by the active support of major computer suppliers. This interest in AI is truly international and is being spurred by various international consortia. Another indication of the magnitude of this interest is the attendance of perhaps 50,000 individuals at a satellite symposium sponsored by a supplier of AI hardware and software. It should be noted that it is not only companies with a strong computer orientation who are developing knowledge systems. For example, consumer products companies are developing and using systems for marketing, scheduling, and planning (Waterman, 1986). Also active are many accounting and management consulting firms.

A system has been developed to assist farmers in selecting grain marketing alternatives. Incorporated in the system are market characteristics and such individual farmer attributes as storage facilities, personal preference on delivery locations, and familiarity with the futures market. A very different type of AI application is an expert system which provides a tutorial in music theory. It features interactive drills and diagnostic advice to the user.

Amidst all this euphoria are some sobering factors. There is a definite need for standards which will accelerate the application of AI technology. Standards are required in such areas as language features, input-output, hardware, interfaces, ability to port software from system to system, communications and data access. Some progress is being made, particularly in the development of standards on reusable AI software modules. There is also a backlash of disappointment. Some extravagant claims have been made for the promise of AI technology, particularly by the nontechnical media. This has inevitably resulted in adverse reaction as the realization appears that there are, indeed, limits to this technology. It will not clone the human brain, at least not for a long time to come (McDermott *et al.*, 1985)! This backlash is subsiding as favorable results of actual and realistic applications are reported.

TRENDS

Several trends may be extrapolated from the increasing familiarity with the application of AI technology. Many people exploiting this technology will use it unknowingly. As in the case of most computer users, these people will have but a limited comprehension of software design theory. Where individual AI modules are marketed, they will readily interface to a vast array of existing software packages, without requiring extensive recoding. For example, large simulation packages will be interfaced with reusable knowledge-processing modules for diagnosis, pattern matching, planning and classification. Use of these sophisticated systems will be greatly facilitated by enhanced speech-recognition capabilities. Although these trends can be predicted as occurring in the near future, they will be paced by the requirements for substantial investments in engineering, marketing and support.

As better software tools become available, there will be an increasing number of applications where the knowledge-system builder need not be a highly competent design engineer. This will be particularly true for small systems where the knowledge elicitation and representation is not complex. In these cases, end users will develop and maintain their own knowledge systems on application-specific shells. The advantage of using such shells will include responsiveness to specialized requirements, competitive leverage and protection of proprietary information.

In addition to rapid advances in hardware and software, progress is being made in overcoming some of the fundamental limitations noted earlier in this chapter. The large potential for AI utilization in realtime systems is spurring many R&D programs. New system and software architectures are being developed (Raulefs *et al.*, 1987). There is a similar motivation for the development of rudimentary learning systems. Close examination of the reported work would suggest that the term "teachable" systems is more appropriate. Some of the reported work on learning can also be related to truth maintenance or debugging techniques that find inconsistencies in a knowledge base. An interesting possibility is the use of examples to develop knowledge systems (Dolan and Dyer, 1985; Salzberg, 1985; Neves, 1985). Rule-induction techniques are being used to learn how to plan by analyzing examples of previously prepared plans (Dechter and Michie, 1984).

In a reversal of roles, a system was designed with an internal induction tool to verify information in its knowledge base that was obtained by elicitation from experts. Another system is being developed that finds requirements for "teaching" or program bugs by comparing the results of rule firings generated by semi-random input to the results of a process simulation running on the same input (Pazzani, 1986). Again, the reader is cautioned to evaluate the significance of "teaching" versus "learning." A somewhat similar concept is being used in a research program which is endeavoring to include elementary common sense in a knowledge base. The researchers are studying how the lack of common sense might cause the system to fail. They then insert additional interrogations and confirmations into the knowledge base. Other approaches to learning are also being studied (Bock, 1986; Chien, 1987; Dolan and Dyer, 1985).

Another interesting research area is reasoning by analogy; simulating human thought processes in a rudimentary manner. The intent is to be able to solve a problem by extrapolation from similar previously solved problems (Elliot, 1986). This is a difficult and challenging area of research; one researcher has estimated that his program will require more than 100 person-years and 8 calendar years to achieve a useful reasoning-by-analogy capability. Eventually, these systems may also possess limited introspection and self-awareness. When such systems begin dispensing advice on critical matters, it may be necessary to establish validating agencies such as the Food and Drug Authority. Should an engineering design program be certified like an engineer? It is interesting to speculate on the eventual capabilities of AI technology. Will there be a fundamental limit to how much AI technology will eventually be able to achieve (Winegard et al., 1985)? There may, indeed, be such a limit, but long before it is reached, AI technology will be employed in many many useful applications.

5

The Market for Artificial Intelligence

ORIGINS

Until the explosion in artificial intelligence of the last five years, the commercial AI market was almost invisible and the military AI market was confined to research and development with a strong academic focus. There were a few nonacademic organizations like Bolt Beranek and Newman (BBN), the Xerox Palo Alto Research Center (PARC) and the Stanford Research Institute (SRI) that had ongoing, primarily federally funded basic research programs and several Federal Research Centers like the Rand Corporation that also worked on various aspects of AI. The major AI research centers were the Massachusetts Institute of Technology (MIT), Carnegie Mellon University (CMU), Yale and Stanford University. The work done in these institutions provided the technology base that fueled the AI explosion that occurred in the 1980s.

The computer of choice for all these institutions was the DEC PDP 10/20 supplemented by various institution-specific machines for LISP processing built at PARC, BBN and MIT and various forms of high-resolution graphic displays.

CURRENT STATUS

The next stage of the market, just now (1987) terminating, was the technology development and investigation market. It started with a lecture-seminar market to meet an almost insatiable demand for information across industry and government. As the technology market grew, nearly all of the hardware and software developments associated with academic and industrial research of any promise were productized and marketed by a number of companies, most formed specifically for the purpose. The purchasers of these products were other AI companies and the R&D components of many American and Asian companies. Industrial AI interest in Europe lagged several years behind other countries, however.

Several aspects of this market must be understood in order to predict the future, or rather to avoid using the parameters of this market as an immediate guide to the future. Since the primary emphasis was on the evaluation of technology and its use to develop more technology, innovative features were more important than immediate gain from use of this technology. Many, if not most, buyers of AI software and hardware were purchasing with the purpose of learning about and then investigating the value of the technology to their firms, not to solve a specific problem. In fact, the organizational context of these buyers was usually R&D, not operations. Thus, there was a powerful force on suppliers to compete on features, not solutions.

If one shell maker offered backward chaining, all had to, because this capability might be needed when training was over, and an application was selected and development actually started. Thus, each shell maker tried to supply the universal system to users who made choices without really knowing if they were correct. Suppliers found that supplying information to naive users was the largest cost component of their products.

Applications were often selected more because of their technologic appeal and demonstration value than for their immediate, bottom-line impact. The application-selection criteria tended to focus on technology and not integration issues.

Frequently, the cost of integration of an AI prototype system can be equal to the development cost of the system itself. Here we mean the connection of a system to realtime corporate sources of information and the use of a delivery environment for the developed system, as opposed to a development environment. Deferring system integration to a later phase provided the maximum visible technologic impact for the funds expended. Integration, while important, was seen as less technically challenging. This attitude affected suppliers as well as buyers. Developing integration capability in a features-competitive marketplace seemed to be a less attractive, as well as less interesting, alternative to the technology innovators who were the driving force in the AI technology supplier firms.

Such an approach is appropriate for the investigation of any new technology, on the part of new users. However, the behavior of this type of market cannot be extrapolated to a more mature situation where cost-benefit trade-offs can be, and are, made on a more immediate basis. In fact, even in a technology-investigation market there may be considerable confusion in objectives when different groups within a company view a particular approach with quite different value systems. As the AI market has matured, this conflict even occurs in the decision process in a large company, where the technology innovators favor a high-technology answer and the operators could not care less, as long as their current problems are solved promptly and at the lowest cost.

The technology-investigation market, as long as it lasted, tended to shield the suppliers of AI technology from the realities of a solution-oriented market focused on low-risk, low-cost solutions. Further, the marketplace that these AI suppliers had positioned themselves to serve is diminishing, as the R&D organizations that had supported it spend budgeted funds and move on to other areas of investigation.

The Federal Government, particularly the Department of Defense, recognized the potential of AI technology for support of decision making, maintenance of complex systems, and execution of hazardous operations, and made heavy investments in both R&D and application development.

Finally, academic institutions, suffering from increased competition and trying to give training in "hot" subjects, have been forming AI departments to provide professional training in the subject.

PROJECTIONS

Forecasting trends in the types of applications that will become the sources of commercial interest in this rapidly changing market can be difficult (and hazardous). However, there are some identifiable factors which should influence the direction that the AI industry will follow.

A new market phase has started that is oriented primarily to solutions rather than technology. In this market, the suppliers of AI technology are dealing with customers who have little interest in any particular technology. Rather, they are almost technology-independent and interested in total solutions. The specialty suppliers of AI technology may no longer be dealing with the ultimate users of their products. Rather, they will supply their products to developers that have the capability to perform systems integration and deliver and support a complete product to the customer. Many of these development organizations exist within companies but, in many cases, these organizations have not been involved with the evaluation of AI technology. In fact, there is probably much negative bias against AI technology in these organizations since they were on the sidelines while all the glory and upper management attention was focused on the AI evaluators. The sales forces of the AI technology companies have had little interaction with these organizations and may not understand the different cultures that exist within them. To deal with this problem, AI technology firms can change their approach or expand their scale of operation to become technology-independent suppliers.

There are other trends likely to occur. In a significant announcement, the world's largest producer of computers, IBM, stated its intention to establish a strong presence in the AI technology market (Schorr, 1986). The main market segment addressed was AI subsystems, imbedded in larger mainframe programs, using an internally developed shell for the purpose. These imbedded subprograms are expected to replace some of the routine tasks performed by system operators and maintenance personnel. IBM envisions this type of expert system as being used in a wide range of limited domain areas, related to the use of mainframes.

There should be a continuing market for the equivalent to the "high-end" program development workstation, although the unit cost of these systems will decline continuously due to learning-curve effects. It may well be that the high-end PC and the low-end program development workstation will become indistinguishable as 32-bit CPU technology permeates the marketplace. The most successful supplier of these systems will develop technology that will minimize the pain associated with transfer of completed programs to delivery systems and maintenance of these programs throughout their life cycle. Current work on automatic programming technology, while not replacing the programmer, should provide the basis for life-cycle programming support. An important part of this technology will be VLSI-based delivery systems that will run development languages efficiently in non-development environments. Another important issue for these vendors will be the development of a low-risk path from a working prototype to an operational system. Users are not anxious to deal with many system-integration problems, accompanied by finger-pointing from several vendors, each with a piece of the action.

The "expert assistant" workstation that uses AI and advanced graphics technology to support data-intensive activity will become a more important factor in the marketplace. These machines will be able to access existing mainframe data bases painlessly and also have VLSI-based graphics interaction capability. Such systems will be used for all types of engineering design activity and will be able to provide limited domain expertise with an expert override capability when the system is used outside its programmed domain.

The "all-purpose" expert system shell may become a less important part of the market in the future. There are several reasons for this; to some extent, the all-purpose shell was a product for the technology evaluation market. The problems with design and maintenance of imbedded control systems in these shells plus their relatively high cost may change customer interest in them. More special-purpose shells will be offered, designed for a particular type of application like planning, chemical process diagnosis, engine maintenance or mechanical design, that can be customized by users in a high-level language. There will be modular components that can be assembled by a user to build a specific product. These components will do such things as inferring (the inference engine), explain, control, organize rules, and interface with data.

VLSI technology will be used to provide language-specific boards for use in existing computers. These boards will ease the delivery system problem, to the extent that current generations of 32-bit CPU's are deemed inadequate. VLSI technology will also provide enhanced graphics capability so that design and publishing activity will not be display-limited. Although current researchers report difficulties, the art of VLSI design will probably advance to a point where firmware will replace software in many applications, thus reducing the copying and piracy problem (Inverson, 1987).

It seems entirely possible that most of the present types of commercial or near-commercial AI systems will soon become part of conventional computer science technology. AI academic research may then emphasize such areas as appplication of massively parallel computers to the currently difficult problems still done most effectively by humans.

What is now called "expert system" technology will be widely used as an integrated part of more conventional software, to handle those rote operations that exist in a limited domain. Thus, design support systems, for mechanical, electrical, chemical and architectural design as well as for software itself, should become much more common. It may also be possible that causal explanation systems will be used for both conventional and AI software systems.

To summarize, vendors will sell solutions, not technology, if they hope to survive in the new market. The use of AI technology will continue to expand, but certainly not in the same manner as in the past.

6

Investment Decisions

BASIS

As noted in Chapter 2, AI technology should have an extensive and positive effect on productivity in business—in how an enterprise functions and in its relation to external forces. However, the development and installation of knowledge systems will typically require substantial capital and other resources. Why, then, should an enterprise make such an investment? A diagramatic representation of trade-offs between investment cost and payback is shown in Figure 6.1. As indicated in the figure, the elements making up the investment cost of the system must be balanced against the potential paybacks. Some of these investment costs, such as capital equipment and staffing, can be estimated with satisfactory precision. Others, such as structural change and long-term maintenance, may be more difficult to quantify. The investment may be justified by improved productivity or enhanced products and services. The possible benefits include:

1. Better and more consistent decision making, across mid-level management

2. Increased capabilities in products or services

3. Reduction of error

4. Reduced time required for product and manufacturing process design

5. Improved training of employees and customers

6. Operational cost savings

7. Better use of the time of a valuable expert

8. More effective management of the intangible asset of collective corporate knowledge

A diverse group of organizations is using AI technology to obtain these benefits. Although there have been demonstrable achievements from the application of AI technology, in many cases it is still difficult to calculate a quantitative payback for the results of this use.

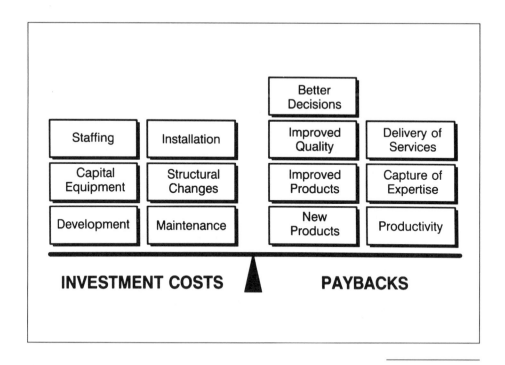

Figure 6.1
Investment Decisions

One senior manager in an organization where evaluation and acting on externally submitted forms was a major activity calculated that an expert system which could handle the easy evaluation (about 30 percent) would allow him to process the expected increase in volume due to planned sales activity without having to hire three additional evaluators. He proved to his management that the expected savings would pay for the system within two years and that the experience gained would permit the system to evolve to handle a much larger percentage of these forms.

Paybacks on an investment may include intangibles. Installation of a knowledge system can be useful in building bridges across organizational components. Once the dynamics of interaction between components have been made explicit, it is easier for managers to make certain that each component is working towards a goal of common benefit. A previous section noted the potential for utilizing natural language front ends on multiple data bases which contain some redundant information. Multifunctional use of such data bases can reduce disputes, and also increase awareness of what each component's functional requirements are and how they may be best satisfied. Another intangible benefit is improved decision making under pressure.

Organizations have received an unexpected benefit during the development of knowledge systems as a result of the knowledge-extraction process. While identifying the knowledge and how it is used, a clearer and mutually understood picture of the internal workings of the organization has been obtained. In fact, there are some instances where this clearer picture resulted in substantial improvement in operations even without the installation of a knowledge system.

Increasing the skills of an employee and utilizing these skills effectively are important corporate investment objectives. How much of that investment is lost when an expert leaves the company by retirement or joins a competitor? Some outstanding successes have been reported in capturing the expertise of a very experienced employee before retirement and then being able to make it available to other employees. Expert systems can also be used to increase the performance of highly skilled professionals and to bring the level of performance of less skilled professionals to a higher common level. Planning personnel are able to consider more complex possibilities and alternatives. Engineers and analysts can create better designs and execute them more efficiently. The creative process is aided by more flexible process simulations or by more complete analysis of the interaction of the design with complex input data—electronic signals, pictorial, written, etc. Overdesign can be reduced while simultaneously increasing safety margins by the use of a system which aids the designer in material and process selection. On the factory floor and in the laboratory, equipment malfunction diagnosis and repair is completed rapidly and accurately. AI technology supports preparation of documentation of expertise or processes which is consistent and less subject to emotional interpretation.

Marketing is a costly and important function for many organizations and AI technology has the potential for improving its effectiveness. AJ technology may be used to develop new product features which previously have been impractical or not cost effective. It may help improve the competitive edge of an organization by increasing productivity in various ways. There have been some expert systems installed by companies in the highly competitive financial services market. Several systems are used to shorten decision making and approval cycle time for granting loans. Some markets already demand that AI technology be used in products and services. More and more Department of Defense Requests For Quotation for new systems development are requiring a demonstration of competence in designing and implementing AI technology as part of the qualification process.

A trend in many markets is the pressure for providing an ever broader range of products. Planners dealing with the resultant increased risk and complexity associated with the development and marketing of a broad product range are being assisted by commercial AI products. Other knowledge-based systems help in maximizing revenues by selecting among an extensive set of pricing alternatives and by providing backup support for bidding decisions. Research and development being done on more perceptive planning systems will assist marketing activities. Such a system, for example, would be capable of interpreting the actions of a competitor and deducing its plans (Kautz and Allen, 1986). Intensifying competition has also brought about a greater awareness of the importance of customer satisfaction. Some of the earliest success stories in artificial intelligence have been from companies that developed AI systems which processed customer orders more accurately and at a lower cost.

STRATEGIES

In considering an investment in AI technology, several strategies may be available to an organization. Possible strategies are indicated in Figure 6.2. Certainly the easiest way is to adopt a wait and see attitude. This may be the easiest way but certainly not the best from a longer-range point of view. An organization may conclude that this technology has not yet had much of an impact in their business. "Why not let a few pioneers spend the money and make the

---

STRATEGIES

- "Wait and See"
- In-house Design
- Consultants
- Universities
- Hardware and Software Suppliers
- Strategic Business Relations

Figure 6.2
Alternatives for Developing AI Systems

mistakes? We'll wait to see how they make out, and then if it makes sense, we'll jump in." This strategy has been satisfactory in some instances in the past, but the rapidly changing business climate makes it a dangerous strategy. A typical knowledge system may require two or three years of development before it can be fielded. In addition, it may take a year to 18 months to build a group with adequate expertise to undertake such a development. The time to catch up to a competitor with a working system that provides real advantages in the marketplace could have adverse competitive consequences.

A second approach is to set up an in-house group to exploit AI technology. If the group is also to be charged with developing AI-based systems, this strategy is perhaps more appropriate for organizations which already have competence in developing computer-based systems. An in-house group has the advantage of protection of proprietary information and may have a focused approach to developing systems which will be specifically responsive to the organization's needs. This group must have a good understanding of how the organization functions, as well as knowledge of its products and services. A disadvantage of this strategy is that it may entail a substantial investment to develop a competent AI group. As noted in subsequent chapters, unusual personnel skills are required as well as specialized development equipment. In order to obtain good results from such a group, it may also be necessary to modify some entrenched concepts, such as crossing organizational boundaries. Specifically, it will be necessary for the group to be closely integrated with those existing organizational components charged with the development and use of computing resources, both hardware and software. Also, the group must be capable of developing real user commitment and support for whatever development work they plan to undertake. Since AI technology is still new and application experience limited, it is wise to have some in-house capability to select suppliers and manage the work on a system that is being developed externally.

If setting up an in-house group is deemed to be impractical or too costly, specialized consultants and universities should be considered. There are a number of consulting groups which have developed a great deal of expertise in designing and installing knowledge systems. Competent consultants have already made the costly investment in training and in gaining field experience. They are aware of the pitfalls and also of the benefits that may be obtained using this technology. Some consultants specialize in assisting an organization to develop its own competence in this area. Other consultants prefer to design a complete system and then turn it over to the customer.

There are trade-offs to be made between having a system developed internally or by a consultant. An important one is whether or not the organization feels that having in-house competence will eventually be an important strategic asset. If so, the investment should be made to build a qualified staff, perhaps with the initial assistance of a consultant. There are, of course, some disadvantages in working with consultants. Initially, they may be totally unaware of the organization's internal and external environment. This may cause delays and misunderstandings and, in more extreme cases, unsatisfactory performance. Competent consultants are much in demand and their services can be quite costly. However, there certainly have been some examples of the high front-end investment returning a good payback. During the complex knowledge-elicitation process, use of consultants may have a distinct advantage; they are less likely to be locked-in by the procedures which have traditionally been used in an organization. In implementing, for example, a system which is to be used internally, they can objectively appraise other approaches. It should be recognized, however, that an organization using outside resources and systems without developing in-house capability is actually making an effective commitment to the supplier for the life of the system.

Many of the AI technology relationships between industrial organizations and universities have been in the support of ongoing research. There have been some instances where industrial organizations have relied on universities to provide the initial development portion of a knowledge system. One of the advantages is that universities are frequently on the cutting edge of the new technology. They are aware of advances in concepts and in implementation methods and usually objective in their recommendations on the hardware or software to be used. Faculty and students may also have high levels of technical competence which would be hard to reproduce in an industrial organization. A potential difficulty is the differences in orientation between the university and an industrial organization. The university is, of course, primarily concerned with teaching and research. The industrial organization typically is more concerned with developing a product or improving a process. As a result, conflicts can arise on schedule and cost commitments, incomplete documents, and on limited support of software. There may also be substantial differences in perception of user needs. An approach which has been effective in some situations is to utilize project-directed university faculty or students working at campus laboratories or on the premises of the industrial organization. Again, care must be exercised in how the development process is managed.

A number of systems have been developed in collaboration with commercial suppliers of AI hardware and software. Some suppliers have extensive experience in using this technology as well as competent development staff. The development cycle is shortened if they already have experience in related applications. They may also be willing to make some concessions on the conditions for acquisition of their hardware or software. The obvious disadvantage to the buyer is in being locked into the use of specific hardware and software before being certain that it is the most appropriate for the application. The hardware or software provided or used by the supplier may turn out to be optimum for the application, but it will be difficult to make any major changes in the system environment once a serious commitment has been made.

If the investment in a custom-designed system is not warranted, another approach is to purchase a fully developed knowledge system. Sophisticated packages or systems are available or are soon to be available for financial applications, manufacturing, planning and many other areas. These packages frequently include many desirable features and provide the advantages noted above for using AI technology. Purchasing such a system could be costly but it could also shorten the time required to begin obtaining the benefits of AI technology. Purchasing a packaged system has competitive implications, i.e., will the organization gain an edge by using this package or will the same package be available to all of the organization's competitors?

Several large organizations have purchased an equity interest in smaller AI companies. This has enabled them to have some level of privileged access to a capability which would have taken them a long time to develop internally. These young AI companies possess skills and an entrepreneurial spirit which would be difficult to duplicate in older and larger organizations. Of course, care must be exercised to make sure that this entrepreneurial spirit is not dampened by association with the large organization.

RESOURCE REQUIREMENTS

If the strategy selected is to buy a packaged system or to make an equity investment, the front-end cost can be reasonably well predicted. (Total cost, however, may not be so easily defined.) Estimating the initial cost for a system to be developed internally is more difficult. As an order of magnitude, an expert system comprising less than 500 rules can be initially developed with a direct labor cost of less than $100,000 by a reasonably skilled group (exclusive of overhead, equipment, and integration costs). A large system can cost ten or twenty times as much. There are wide variations in these figures; additional "yardsticks" are discussed in Chapter 12. If the development and installation of a knowledge system is to remain the responsibility of the organization, then a number of investments must be made. Resources primarily consisting of skilled personnel and specialized equipment must be acquired. Chapter 12 discusses staffing requirements and Chapter 15 discusses development hardware and software. There are trade-offs between development-time cycles and personnel assignments to the project, but care must be exercised in not taking too many financial shortcuts in providing the necessary development environment. In making investment estimates, another cost to be considered is the effort involved in technology transfer. This effort may entail integrating the system into the corporate culture, organizational relationships, conversion from prototype to delivered system, user training, and connecting the system to sources of on-line data. The type of application also has a strong bearing on the investment that must be made. A system intended to become part of a military product with stringent reliability requirements or a system for real-time control of a process will have a higher development cost than a consumer product.

PAYBACKS

In addition to the initial impressive achievements at Digital Equipment Corporation, a few other reports have emerged on AI projects which have demonstrated good (and measurable) paybacks. In one proprietary program, a company easily implemented a knowledge system. The system was developed at a cost of $65,000 and is credited with generating savings of $1.5 million. Another company developed an electronic circuit diagnostic system in four months. This system is stated to be capable of identifying 98 percent of faults occurring in manufacturing with an accuracy level approaching 100 percent. It has almost eliminated the replacing of boards which are not actually defective. Total savings are estimated to be $5 million annually.

These results are impressive, but at this early phase in the evolution of AI, there are relatively few fielded systems for which financial results have been verified. As yet, there are not many instances where the number of dollars saved or reduced number of employees required to perform a function have been documented. It can also be difficult to extrapolate the results obtained in one application to those which might be obtained in a different application. Still, if a decision maker is asked to invest a million dollars and ten person-years to field a knowledge system, it is quite legitimate to ask about a return on investment.

As noted previously, some of the paybacks and benefits of this technology are intangible. They may derive from:

Exploitation of new technology and procedures by:

- Capturing and enhancing knowledge.
- Developing new products.
- Improving process efficiency.
- Supporting experts.

Consider the following examples of good potential applications for knowledge systems whose payback and benefit would be difficult to quantify:

1. An adviser to aid a human in responding to situations which occur infrequently or as a result of an unusual combination of circumstances.

2. An analytic or diagnostic tool which reduces the unanticipated downtime of expensive assets.

3. A product design aid which reduces the time required to get a product to the market.

4. A knowledge-elicitation and codifying process which results in a better understanding of the organization's "inner workings" and how they might be improved.

These benefits are quite real, but it is difficult to put a price tag on them. If these difficult to quantify benefits are not included in ROI calculations, then they are essentially being assigned a value of zero. In order to avoid this inaccuracy, a value for these benefits should be estimated in order to compute a relevant ROI. Perhaps a different measurement of return on investment should be utilized. The consideration could be potential business which is gained or lost; access to a new market segment; a lowered cost of doing business; etc. An adherence to rigid accounting methods may result in lost opportunities.

7

Knowledge and Its Management

OVERVIEW

This chapter provides a pragmatic view of knowledge, particularly from the viewpoint of industry, that may assist a manager in understanding the possible benefits available to an organization from application of AI-based knowledge-management techniques.

One of the unexpected results of applied work on AI over the last few years has been the recognition that it is both possible and desirable to consider the knowledge of the work force in a company and the possible implementation of elements of that knowledge in a computer system as separate items. Once this view is adopted, it is possible to evaluate and use what is learned during knowledge elicitation, impartially and appropriately.

TYPES OF KNOWLEDGE

Members of the AI Center at Arthur D. Little, Inc. have developed some concepts of considerable assistance in understanding

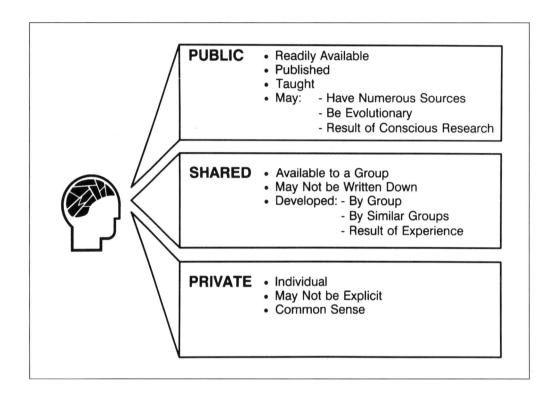

Figure 7.1
Views of Knowledge

the types of knowledge that might be encountered within a company and how to use this knowledge to its benefit. Although generalizations are not necessarily accurate, it is sometimes useful to make general statements for clarification. With this caveat, we generalize about the nature of knowledge, how it is acquired and how it can be elicited, to assist the reader in understanding the points made in this chapter.

Knowledge may be classified into three general categories of increasing abstraction or generalization: public, shared and private, as shown in Figure 7.1.

1. Public knowledge is generally available in the most explicit and abstract forms. It can be taught in schools and expressed as algorithms. Its application and dependencies are generally well bounded and understood mutually within groups of experts trained in its use.

2. Shared knowledge is developed as part of the environment of a group who work or interact together. It is, in general, less abstract in nature. This type of knowledge may not be written down in any formal way but is commonly held within the group and can be described, or at least used as a basis, for common interaction by the members of the group. Team sports and construction crews operate with shared knowledge (Kidder, 1986).

3. Private knowledge is totally individual. It is usually based on the experiences of the individual and provides a structure for the solution of problems and individual actions. This type of knowledge is often, in fact, generally indescribable by the individual who possesses it, if elicited under conditions that are conceptually removed from the conditions where it is normally used. Special techniques are needed to access this private knowledge and develop a formal structure for organizing and describing it.

Private knowledge and "common sense" are closely equivalent and the difficulty of obtaining such knowledge is one reason why the literature on building expert systems suggests that it is better to avoid applications where "common sense" is needed to solve problems. Private knowledge seems to be the least abstract form of knowledge in the context we are describing it since it is specific to both individuals and circumstances.

As shown in Figure 7.2, there is another dimension of increasing abstraction that can be used for the description of knowledge. This dimension describes the content rather than the nature of knowledge and is actually more complex than can be shown in the two dimensions of Figure 7.2. Facts, data and observations are

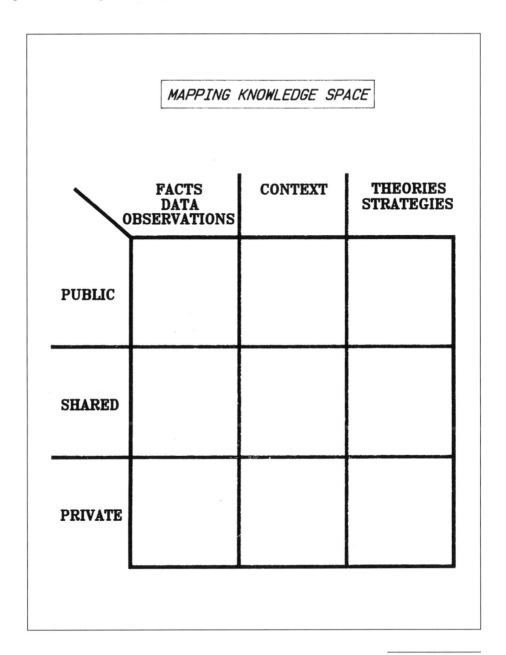

Figure 7.2
Mapping Knowledge Space

specific and are supposedly, at least, observer-independent. They have the lowest degree of abstraction. Context is a more judgmental evaluation and is used by the observer to qualify the facts and other generally known observables. The term "context" also includes the evaluation of the specific environment in which facts exist and is at a higher level of abstraction. Finally, theories or strategies are used by an individual to relate facts and contexts where a specific mechanism may or may not be explicit. This is the highest level of abstraction. In another sense, however, theories can be thought of as a specific formulation of a series of observations, so there is a form of recursion along this dimension as well. Probably Figure 7.2 should be three dimensional and folded on itself.

To obtain an idea of the power of context recognition in human intelligence and the effect of its lack, it is suggested that the reader review some of the literature on brain-damaged patients (Sacks, 1985).

The development of a new field of knowledge can be outlined with Figure 7.3 as a basis. Development of a new set of ideas starts at the lower left corner and spreads, inductively, toward the upper right, although, because of the recursive nature of the horizontal dimension of the figure, some of the initial development would also spread deductively upward from the lower right.

As the depth of understanding of the new field increases, growth occurs both from the bottom right and left, leaving the context sensitivity of specific applications to be held as private and shared knowledge. On the other hand, as shown in Figure 7.4, the design of a knowledge-based software system would most likely start at the upper left and spread, also inductively, downwards and towards the lower right to include more expert knowledge as the system grew more complex. So far, it has been difficult to add additional theoretical or deep knowledge to such an expert system except as specific processes that are algorithmic in nature and do not really "know" anything about the data that they operate on. These models demonstrate, perhaps, the difference in approach between that used by an "expert" in learning about a new area in the first place and that of the system developer, who starts with the most algorithmic aspects of knowledge and only lastly, if ever, uses personal and private knowledge.

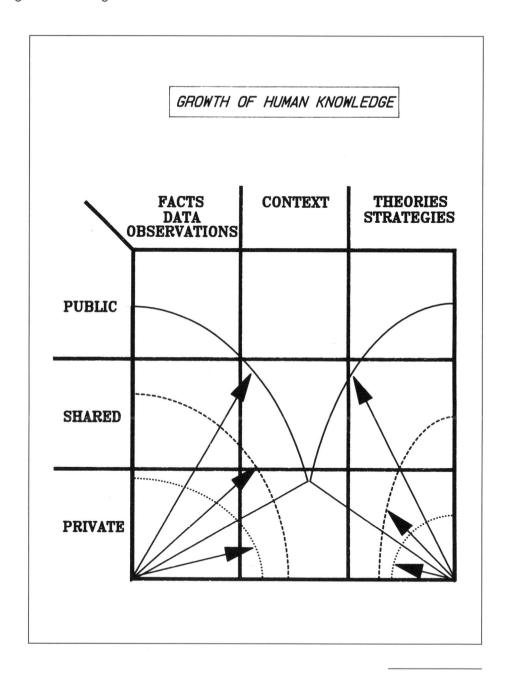

Figure 7.3
Growth of Human Knowledge

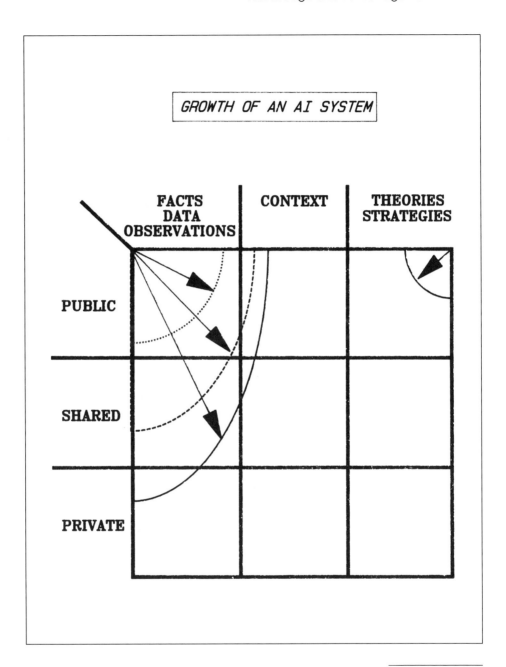

Figure 7.4
Growth of an AI System

NATURE OF EXPERIENCE

Most of us develop our private knowledge on the basis of experience, over time, in various situations. The distribution of the types of knowledge we possess and use is a function of that body of experience. We apparently accumulate experience in various contexts and solve problems by recognizing the appropriate context and extrapolation strategy to employ in order to draw on our experience base. This experience base appears to be quite different among different classes of individuals and can result in strong and sometimes troublesome interaction across experience classes if not recognized and dealt with specifically. Some examples of this point follow, but much work remains to be done before these concepts can be regarded as well understood.

One type of experience-based knowledge is found among plant operators, say in the chemical industry. Many expert chemical plant operators, in one sense, "understand" the behavior of their plants well, such understanding having been obtained over many years of experience with the plant. This understanding is completely different from the "understanding" of the engineers who designed the plant and have responsibility for its operation.

Most experienced operators view the plant as a black box with which they interact. Each operator probably has only rudimentary, or even erroneous, knowledge of the descriptions of the physical and chemical processes that are the primary basis of the knowledge of the design engineer. However, the public and shared knowledge used by the design engineer should be also recognized as containing approximations, developed over time on the basis of theory and practice, to actual conditions in the plant. These approximations are used because they provide satisfactory results. Actually, the knowledge of operators probably contains much of the effective difference between the algorithmic approximations used by designers and the actual conditions and effects in the plant processes.

Capturing this knowledge and merging it with algorithmic or causal knowledge can provide improved insight into both the actual processes and what are required to operate them well. It also preserves an important capital asset of a corporation that has usually been obtained at considerable cost in time and lost production, material and labor. Current techniques of training are more likely to focus on handbook conditions and miss important empirical techniques used by senior operators and which may or may not be acquired by new operators during on-the-job experience. The techniques for capture and explication of private knowledge are still on the primitive side but should evolve rapidly in the next few years. As these techniques evolve, the capture and use of private knowledge in the work force of a company will become a more routine practice with benefit to both design and operations.

As mentioned previously, the considerable difference in viewpoint between those who are primarily holders of private knowledge, such as plant operators, and holders of public knowledge, such as design engineers, can be a source of considerable tension.

At a meeting where the concept of private knowledge of operators and its potential value to a company was being explained, a senior executive/engineer, who had design responsibility for chemical plants, heatedly denied that there was any such thing as private knowledge to be found in any of "his" plants.

The knowledge elicitor should also be aware that this tension can interfere with the elicitation process.

On one occasion, when knowledge was sought from operators who obviously had private knowledge, the plant engineers present refused to allow the operators to talk to the interviewers. Special measures were necessary to get over this hurdle.

BUILDING KNOWLEDGE MODELS AND SYSTEMS

Chapters 11 and 12 detail the various phases of planning, managing, and implementing the design and delivery of a knowledge

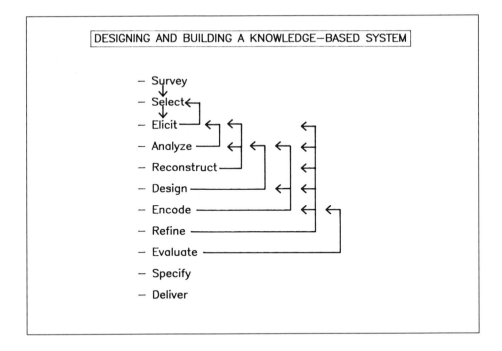

Figure 7.5
Designing and Building a Knowledge-Based System

system. This section focuses on the knowledge elicitation and modeling part of the entire process. As might be expected in a book of this nature, this description is not intended as a tutorial for the apprentice knowledge engineer. Rather it is intended for the manager who needs an overall view of the process to evaluate its potential benefit to the firm or operation. Little has yet been published on this topic in the AI literature although considerable information on interviewing techniques can be found in the ethnographic literature (Spradley, 1979).

    Figure 7.5 lists the various steps in the process of building a knowledge-based system. The process, as shown in the figure, is actually highly recursive. As each step in the process is carried out, the need for additional input from earlier stages in the process

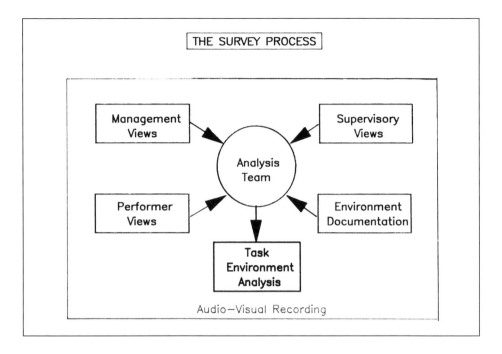

Figure 7.6
The Survey Process

becomes more explicit. The turned arrows show the most common recursive stages. The specific steps in the process are discussed in more detail in later sections of the book.

ENVIRONMENTAL SURVEY

Figure 7.6 shows an overall view of the first step in knowledge elicitation. The object is to determine whether an initial belief that an area contains knowledge which can be captured is correct, to find the primary locations where that knowledge exists and learn how it is employed, and to obtain an idea of a possible system that might be developed to use the knowledge. Some early rules of thumb about the criteria to be used in the selection of "suitable" AI problems are less applicable than the existing literature might indicate. In particular, as long as there is consensus that there is a body of expertise, whether concentrated in a single individual or distributed among several, and that this expertise is routinely used for decision making, knowledge elicitation with the primary objective of automation is likely to pay off.

Seasoned software engineers are likely to find considerable commonality in the description given here and their own experience with existing software development techniques. Experience in the development of conventional software indicates also that there are important differences in emphasis in the techniques described here and the value of this different emphasis should be considered with an open mind.

One of the authors was a member of a team that was doing knowledge engineering in a technical area that was also the subject of an extensive development of a conventional data-base system. The individual responsible for preparation of the specifications for this system was invited to attend the knowledge-engineering sessions. Well into the proceedings, this individual stated that he found his attendance extremely useful since he was hearing about important things that had not been mentioned during several years of developing specifications with the same people involved in knowledge engineering.

There are several objectives for this survey process. The first objective is shown schematically in Figure 7.7, to identify those areas whose knowledge content is sufficiently rich as to justify focused knowledge elicitation. Figure 7.8 gives some rules that can be used to evaluate the suitability of a specific area for implementation of a knowledge-based system. Basically, these rules are derived from the experience of others (Waterman, 1986), but have been revised to include the personal experience of ourselves and our colleagues. In most cases, there is general agreement that there are some persons, usually more than one, who possess "expertise." It is less clear at the start what the nature of this "expertise" is. For practical reasons, it seems better to find expertise that is used in a

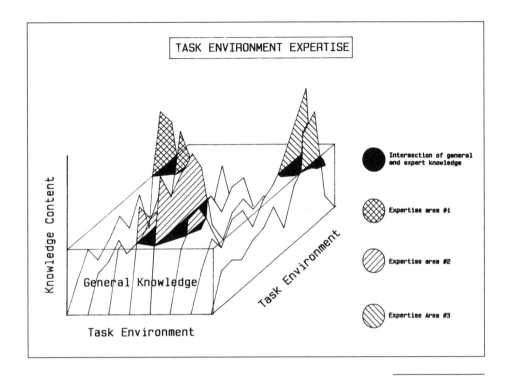

Figure 7.7
Task Environment Expertise

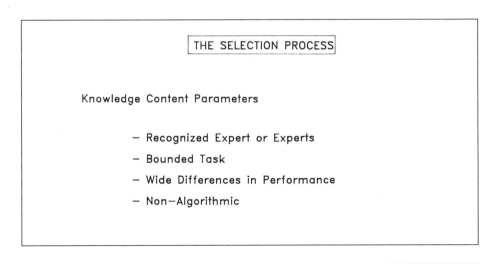

Figure 7.8
The Selection Process

bounded task. If the task seems to be large and extend over a long period of time, it is likely that a number of bounded subtasks can be found within the large task and which should be analyzed individually.

In cases where the existence of "expertise" is not recognized, another selection criteria is that there is a considerable difference in the time or quality of performance between different individuals who perform the same task. Finally, it is worthwhile to look for a strong algorithmic content to the task. If such an algorithmic content is present, it may be useful to consider conventional technology for automation of the task. Some of the rules recommended in other texts have been omitted from the list in Figure 7.8. This omission is deliberate, since we have found that our techniques support the implementation of a wider range of applications than have been practical in the past.

The second objective of the survey is to obtain a detailed understanding of the environment which surrounds the knowledge to be elicited. There will be many different views of this environment and it is important to obtain these views and synthesize them into a unified whole. This synthesis will include the nature of the expert task to be performed, its source and the use of its results. The elicitor should also establish the artifacts of the task such as language, symbols, types of external knowledge, and how and from where they are obtained. Finally, it is necessary to determine and evaluate the participation of others in the task.

A third objective of the survey is to obtain enough information about the environment in which the task is performed so that it will be possible to evaluate the changes that might result in the work environment if some or all elements of a task area were automated. This evaluation is of considerable importance to make both available and explicit the probable impact of the completed system in the early stages of the task-selection process. If this explication were delayed until a prototype be completed there might well be a considerable morale problem as those concerned begin to recognize the effect of a new capability on the existing work environment. In several cases, work on a prototype had to be stopped because of unanticipated intense reactions of those concerned.

A final objective of the survey is to select the intellectual approach to be used in design of the system. Early publicity associated with expert systems suggested that replacement of human activity by a computerized system was possible and it was just a matter of extracting the rules from an expert and implementing them in a particular system. (The possible dental analogy associated with the word "extracting" in this instance is deliberate on the part of the authors.) Experience shows it is difficult to replace the context recognition and implementation strategy of humans in anything but a toy system and so the idea of an intelligent assistant rather than a replacement is more appropriate for most useful applications.

Figure 7.6 suggests that all organizational levels surrounding the area of interest should be consulted during the survey. Because the time of the individuals involved is valuable and much of the necessary information can be obtained only by careful analysis, complete audiovisual records of all interviews should be made, if possible.

KNOWLEDGE ELICITATION

Given that areas of high and valuable knowledge content have been identified in an environmental survey, the next task is to elicit the knowledge contained in these areas. The environmental survey will have identified the general location and type of most of the public material that is used for the performance of the task, but it is necessary to have access to most of the material that is used for day-to-day reference by those who work in the selected area as part of the elicitation process. During this part of the process it is necessary to meet a number of requirements. An obvious one is to establish an effective working relationship with the expert. Considerable sensitivity may be required. It is quite probable that the elicitor is asking for a condensed version of a lifetime of experience, the components of which are the primary source of economic and professional security for the individual concerned. An attitude of respectful listening is recommended. The results of the elicitation will be included in a knowledge model, so it is important to obtain the various aspects of the knowledge process that the expert uses. The main elements include:

1. Symbols and language used

2. Organization and structure of knowledge

3. Elements of knowledge

4. Reasoning methods used

5. Knowledge sources

6. Products or results provided

7. Examples or test cases for use in evaluation

The elicitor should not expect that most experts can provide a complete output of their knowledge in the orderly and logical form described above. These elements are given as a mental checklist that the elicitor can use to structure the interviews tactfully so as to arrive at a more or less complete coverage of the important elements. In fact, the expert may not even be capable of recognizing, initially at least, the reorganized and structured version of the elicited knowledge.

One knowledge elicitor was requested to have the final product of the elicitation and organization process "checked by the expert." The initial result was quite disheartening for the elicitor because the expert immediately denied that each element of the product was right. Consistently, however, after an interval of several minutes, the expert would interrupt the discussion of the next element and confirm the correctness of the previous element. The ex post facto explanation for this, given by the elicitor, was that it was necessary for the expert, whose knowledge was organized as a series of experiences, to translate and relate each element to a past experience that verified the content of the element in the frame of reference of the expert.

Figure 7.9 shows an idealized approach to be used to obtain the individual knowledge of each of the experts involved in the

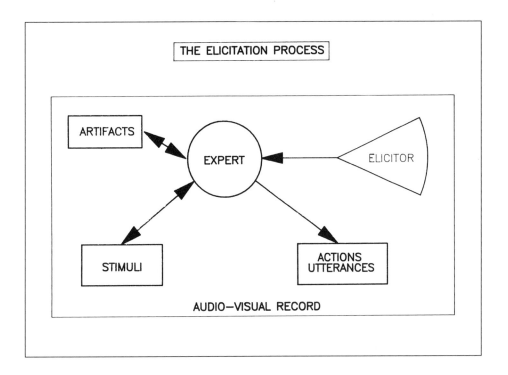

Figure 7.9
The Elicitation Process

selected area. The expert responds to stimuli with the use of expertise and refers to artifacts to supplement his or her knowledge.

The methods of knowledge elicitation to be used in a specific circumstance can vary with the nature of the expertise and the explanation skills of the knowledge holder. For public and shared knowledge, it is sometimes possible to use more or less standard interviewing techniques. If the knowledge is private or based on experience, it may be necessary to use an evoked response to stimulus technique, where the expert is asked to talk ("think aloud") about his or her thoughts and actions as a task is performed with new input data. Retrospective analysis of the process of a previously performed task is likely to give incorrect results relative to the actual knowledge and expertise that is used. There seems to be a need for rationalization of expertise in a retrospective mode that is destructive to the initial content. In most cases, at least initially, there is a need to use both audio and visual recording methods, since the expert may point or look at a specific item or information source that would not be deducible from what was said.

The elicitor role may actually be shared among several individuals since, as will be seen, it can be quite complex. One responsibility is that of the sympathetic and understanding listener. The expert should feel that his or her expertise is understood, and appreciated in a noncompetitive way. Although this is still a subject of debate, some experts feel that their time is being wasted if the elicitor appears totally ignorant of their field and every term and issue must be explained at an elementary level. On the other hand, such elementary explanation can sometimes reveal important aspects of knowledge that are concealed in jargon and "mutually understood" concepts. Desirable characteristics of the elicitor or knowledge engineer are discussed in Chapter 11.

Another responsibility might be described as the keeper of the data dictionary. This role requires explication, by questioning the expert, at an appropriate time, of the meaning of terms, symbols and other markers of specific concepts and meanings.

A final responsibility is the general conduct of the elicitation process to be sure that important points are covered, that the expert is comfortable and forthcoming and that the elicited information is properly recorded.

One person should have the responsibility for camera operation if video recording is used; particularly if the situation is dynamic so that a fixed camera orientation does not cover the action. Frequently, zooming will be needed to resolve a particular work space.

We have found that more than one elicitor is appropriate, but that the nature of the individuals on the knowledge-elicitation team and their capabilities can be the basis for *ad hoc* assignment of roles.

KNOWLEDGE ANALYSIS

The next step in the knowledge capture process is shown in Figure 7.10. This step is still a highly individual and personal process and perhaps will remain so in the future, since considerable

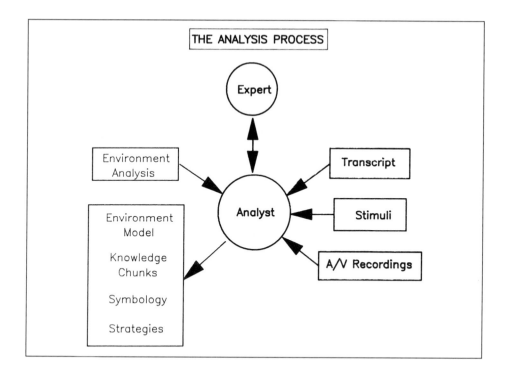

Figure 7.10
The Analysis Process

creativity is required. As is shown, the objective of this stage of the process is to take all the fragments of knowledge and the artifacts that are associated with them that have been gathered; create an architecture that can contain this data; and then assemble the available material into a model of the knowledge and process used by the performers of a task that can be used for system development. One primary input to this process is a transcript of the utterances of the expert during the elicitation process. The term "utterances" has been chosen deliberately to reflect the complexity of the analysis. The analysis process is quite labor-intensive, and may require as much as ten hours of analysis for every hour of elicitation.

In preparation for this analysis, a transcription of the utterances of the expert must be made. The transcription task itself requires special training, such as for transcription of courtroom testimony. Sentences may be incomplete and the most important words are often spoken with the least clarity. Ordinary secretarial training and motiation is <u>not</u> adequate. A full day of interviewing will result in about 400 pages of double-spaced text.

Basically, the analyst/designer must take each paragraph in the transcript, interpret the vague references, extract the content and associate this paragraph content with other related "chunks" of knowledge that have been obtained previously. This process may require reference to video recordings, artifacts or any other sources of pertinent information, both to relate external facts to the transcript content and to explicate when the expert is pointing to or using such facts.

As the knowledge chunks are being extracted and ordered, the analyst must be developing the architecture for a knowledge model that will contain and relate the knowledge in a unified whole. The model structure selected will be tempered by the analyst's knowledge of available representation methods. In many cases, it is useful to use one of the commercial knowledge representation shells to support this process since these shells have pre-developed representation methods as well as useful tools for the visualization of relationships within the model structure. Shells are described in Chapter 13.

This discussion, for the purposes of clarity, has separated the various steps in the designing and building of a knowledge system as if they occurred in a totally serial manner. The process is, in fact, usually much more parallel and recursive, as was indicated in Figure 7.5. Thus, the inferring or control capability (inference engine) built into a commercial shell can be used to develop a preliminary system design that can become a powerful knowledge-eliciting tool for the expert, as well as reducing the effort that would be required to develop a more customized tool that might prove to be unsatisfactory later. On the other hand, the representation structure in the tool can influence, perhaps in an undesirable way, the architecture of the developed model.

Another possible approach is to provide the experts with tools that will permit them to enter the rules that represent knowledge directly. In most cases, such an approach should be used after the initial architecture is defined and the expert is polishing the system, rather than developing it from the start. Despite the glowing words of some shell makers, there is a considerable amount of hard thinking required to formulate the detailed structure of a rule-based logical system and there is no reason to believe, in advance, that an expert in a specific field possesses this skill. It is likely that a separate and relatively foolproof system should be developed for use by the expert that only supports minor modifications in knowledge and process control.

There is a famous example of an expert system shell, fairly widely quoted at the time of its initial development, that allowed the expert to enter rules directly as they occurred to him. A developer of the system disclosed that, actually, the rules entered by the expert were not put into the system directly but rather were trapped and later used by a skilled programmer as the basis for changing the system.

Once the analysis process is complete, then it is necessary to assemble the results of this analysis into a coherent whole that can

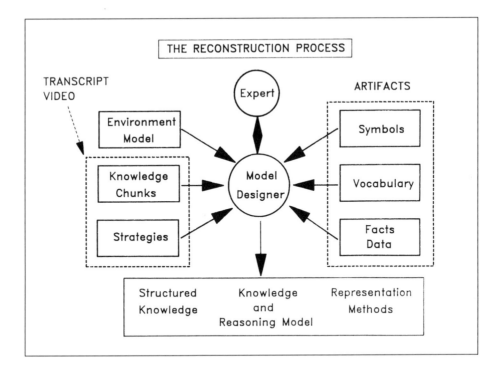

Figure 7.11
The Reconstruction Process

be used as the basis for system design. This part of the process is shown in Figure 7.11, where a model of the knowledge and reasoning processes that are used in the area selected for analysis is built. This model contains the elicited knowledge in an organized structure to support the building of an automated system that will make it available for use.

As was pointed out earlier, the model created sometimes makes it obvious that there is a nonautomated and more cost-effective solution to the requirement for the knowledge-based system.

It is still an open question as to whether some parts of the knowledge-reconstruction process can be either automated or delegated to technicians with a lower level of capability. As more experience is gained in this process, the answer to the question will be more obvious.

KNOWLEDGE-SYSTEM DESIGN

Figure 7.12 shows an outline of a knowledge-system design process. A more detailed description of the entire process is provided in Chapter 11. Obviously, this part of developing a knowledge-based system is similar to that used for conventional software. There are several major differences, however. First, since the overall process is quite recursive, there is a much greater probability that much of the initial system design work will be repeated, perhaps several times, until the knowledge-system design has converged on an effective and efficient architecture. Thus, the normal requirements, specification and design process may be inefficient until the system design has stabilized to a considerable extent. There is a happy medium between anarchy and total specification that the manager of the process must create. As more experience is gained, standardized techniques for this stage of the process will be developed.

A second issue is the need for much greater attention to the user interface. This need arises because of the more symbolic and experiential nature of much of the knowledge that may be contained in the system. We have seen several cases where this requirement was slighted. The system, as originally introduced, was received with acclaim but fell into disuse once the original excitement died

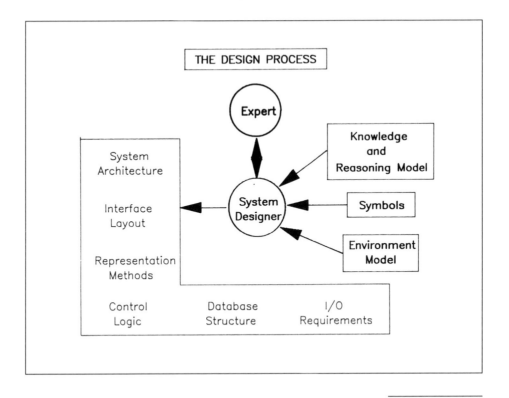

THE DESIGN PROCESS

Figure 7.12
The Design Process

down. It seems as though the technology should be capable of making the often misused term "user friendly" a reality. If the logic and symbols of the interface match the thought patterns of the user, there should actually be no need for an instruction manual for the system.

The final and most important issue is the need for the design of an effective control logic for the system. Logic design must be performed both in the designing and encoding phases of system development. It is difficult to anticipate all the control needs until the system is robust enough that an expert can test its behavior and stress its control logic. Thus, the following discussion applies to both the design and encoding phases of system development described in this and the following section.

The designer must provide for behavior of a much more complex nature than in a conventional system. The selection of the logical subprocess to be next implemented is dependent on the context that is currently appropriate and on past behavior and data. It should be noted that the ability of a human to recognize a particular context and the appropriate strategy to be used in this context is particularly difficult to reproduce in more than a very limited sense with existing technology. This problem is not well covered in the literature that extols the wonders of expert systems, because it was assumed in this literature that the rule base in such a system has general application in all situations in which it would be used.

Further, since combinational explosion is an always present problem in a moderately complex system, limiting the search space while not losing reasoning power is not yet a mature technology. The limitation of search space has been the subject of extensive investigation for some years but considerable art is still required, depending primarily on the nature of the knowledge area under development (Pearl, 1983).

A requirement that must be met with even the simplest of expert systems is the provision of apparent "knowledge" of the meaning of symbols, words or information that have been already been provided to the system. The programmer must provide "artificial wisdom" as control loops which will give the appearance that the system actually understands the meaning of what it has been told, rather than simply matching a supplied text string with a stored equivalent. Efficient recognition of meaning might prove to be an interesting field for research on natural language processing. The recognition space for the meaning of supplied information might be sufficiently limited so as to be within the processing capability of existing systems, whereas the recognition of unlimited free text is not.

ENCODING

Figure 7.13 outlines the encoding process. Because of the requirements for control-logic development and the provision of apparent "intelligence" in the system, the designer and the encoder must

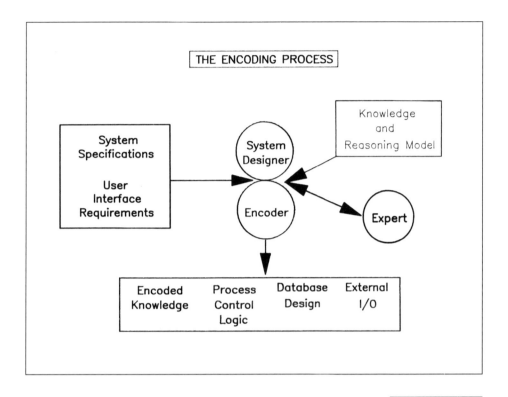

Figure 7.13
The Encoding Process

work closely together. Once the system is sufficiently mature that it can be demonstrated without an instant crash, the expert can be an immediate source of help in finding and fixing system deficiencies and problems. Because of the probability that the system will undergo several major changes during early development, there is a temptation to reduce the amount of effort devoted to some of the more "prosaic" aspects of code development like specifications, documentation and careful testing. Within reason, such an approach makes sense. However, at some point in development, a more ordered and conventional approach is indicated. As more experience is gained, it is likely that standard methods and procedures for rapid development of prototypes will be developed. At present, there is not such a procedure and a manager is responsible for insuring that a sensible balance is reached between the two extremes of laissez faire and a highly ordered development method. (The role of the project manager is more fully discussed in Chapter 11.)

It should be expected that early stages of the development cycle for a knowledge-based system may be shorter in chronological time but may be more complex. First, the prototype itself may be the most important knowledge-eliciting tool. When used by an expert, the prototype will, by its deficiencies, make more explicit the knowledge that is missing or improperly represented. Second, it is likely that the behavior of the typical user will change when the new system is available, thus requiring modification of the knowledge-based system to accommodate such changes. Thus the manager should expect and plan for a stabilization period of 6 to 18 months while a prototype system is in limited use. Pending the availability of low-cost machines that can run development code directly, this stabilization period may demand either the use of high-end machines for prototype delivery or continued expensive code modification in a delivery environment.

COMPLETION

The methodology for implementing an AI project is discussed in Chapter 12. Some elements of this methodology are also discussed in this section since they influence the initial system design.

Once the system has stabilized, it can be transferred to a delivery machine. One definition of stabilization is when the user requests that a recently removed feature be reinstalled. It is probably true that it will be difficult to be certain that the performance of a system is adequate until it has been used under most or all the conditions that will be encountered in its final form. A detailed discussion of this subject belongs in a more technical book, but there are certain points to be made. If the prototype has been written in a high-end development environment, it is certainly operationally functional to a considerable extent but it may be difficult to transfer this functionality easily to a suitable delivery environment directly. As personal computers become more powerful, such transfer may become less of a problem, but in the meantime it is necessary to carry out a fairly sophisticated life cycle cost analysis to develop a correct basis for a delivery environment. It is easy to focus on the first cost of a delivery machine as the most significant item though, of course, cost is a political as well as a technical factor in the decision process. It should be expected that one of the advantages of a knowledge-based system is that its evolution over time, as both knowledge and operating conditions change, is a potential benefit that should be supported. Thus, a process for such evolution should be considered and provided for.

Another factor to consider is the degree of automation provided in the environment where the knowledge-based system is used. If the knowledge-based system is a new automation venture in an area where computer-based support has not been available, it is likely that additional, non-AI computer applications can provide viable and important support for current manual tasks. The nature of these applications, and how to support them, should be considered in the design of the delivery system.

In one application, an expert system was suggested for correction of process control problems in a plant where there were no computers at all. Examination of the process indicated that automation of one of the fundamental process operations would probably remove most of the problems that prompted installation of the expert system in the first place.

Validation, verification and maintenance may be more serious problems with a knowledge-based system than with a conventional system as discussed in Chapter 12. Most non-AI applications have the flow of control reasonably defined by the programmer in advance. In most AI technology applications, the flow of control is imbedded in the rules and procedures, and is both data and data-time-order driven. Most large knowledge-based systems are debugged by brute force and because of the complexity of the internal control structure it is difficult to predict the effect of any change in the internal structure of the program. This comment is not intended to discourage the use of the powerful concepts that have been developed for implementation of knowledge-based systems, but rather to point out the need for the continuing use of high-quality development environments throughout the life cycle of an operational system. The above problems should be better bounded and easier to solve as operating experience with this technology increases.

DATA RECORDING

It is very important to make complete audiovisual recordings of all interviews where knowledge capture is required. If such techniques are not used, it is far too easy to substitute the ideas of the listener for those of the expert source of knowledge being interviewed. The techniques we describe are most intensively used during specific knowledge sessions but apply equally well to some parts of the initial phases of the environmental survey. The home video systems of the VHS stereo high-fidelity, high-quality type have proved to be entirely satisfactory with the added advantage of low cost and light weight. The critical item in the making of effective recordings is usually placement of the microphone to obtain an acceptable signal-to-noise ratio for the audio portion. We have used directional microphones and have also wired the expert with a portable microphone on one channel. It should be noted that a good portable microphone system can cost as much as a complete VHS camera recorder chain. We usually supplement the VHS system with pocket microcassette recorders. These high-end systems will record all participants in a meeting with good fidelity as long as the noise ambient is reasonable and can be used directly for transcription in professional transcription machines. Each microcassette is good for three hours of recording, so that the equipment and supplies for a day's recording can be carried easily in a pocket.

It is important to select, as much as possible, a good environment for making recordings. The human ear is far better at noise discrimination than the automatic volume control system on a recorder and it is easy to make worthless recordings under apparently acceptable conditions. Blowers and air conditioning systems are particularly troublesome sources of noise. Checking and monitoring recordings as they are made can save significant embarrassment. If a separate color monitor is used with the video recorder, it is possible to insure that the color balance is correct and that focus, framing and magnification are suitable. In addition, the camera operator can use the monitor to control the camera from a sitting position so that the recording process is much less conspicuous to the subjects. In general, the entire recording process becomes unnoticed in about ten minutes if the techniques described above are used.

8

Selecting an Appropriate Project

CHOOSING THE RIGHT PROBLEM

Since the field of AI is still in an early stage of maturity, the broad potential applicability of its technology does not diminish the importance of selecting the right series of applications as an organization gains experience in its use. Such selection is vital to the future of subsequent AI programs (and the manager making the selection) as well as to the success of the proposed application. Enthusiasm, as important as it is, must be related to reality. Vendor pre-sale promises must be carefully evaluated. Cost estimates and schedules must be bounded. What can be achieved within the constraints that exist for the program? Careful thought and analysis are required. The application which may appear to offer, for example, the greatest improvement in productivity may not be the best initial project.

After studying numerous possibilities, a manager at a large industrial company concluded that an AI-based assistant for developing conventional software programs offered great promise for improved productivity. However, after studying her

*own company's environment, she decided to put the program-
mers assistant aside and selected a factory test application for
the first project. The manager understood the inner workings of
her company and wisely concluded that a factory test bed would
be a more saleable item for a first project. Improving the
production test of a critical component would have much greater
impact on the "check signers." It was also a much less ambitious
project that could be used to show a payoff at an earlier stage of
completion.*

Conversely, even though a project may be easily saleable, its
scope may strain available resources. Replacing the operating system
of an entire factory is too ambitious for an early effort. Understanding
AI technology is important; understanding the organization's procedures, needs and its tolerance for risk is even more important.

The ensuing discussion describes how to select a project which
will eventually become an external or internal product, rather than
describing procedures for selecting an exploratory R&D project. (The
latter type of project requires different criteria.) There is already
considerable information on the methodology for selecting and carry-
ing out an exploratory project and the potential value of the technology
has already been proved to a point where further investigation is not
really cost-effective in most areas. Parameters relating to project
selection are noted in Figure 8.1. This figure lists some of the sources
of ideas or suggestions for the selection of an AI project. Some of these
sources, such as a customer or domain expert, may not even be part of
the established development organization. The figure also gives some
of the criteria that should be considered when selecting the most
appropriate project from these sources of ideas.

What are some of the methods by which an application area will
be selected? It may be by management direction or it may be selected
by a task force which has been given responsibility for studying several
areas of interest. Both approaches are valid. In fact, it may be well to
use both mechanisms for the first few projects, since the initial
applications chosen may fall outside the normal decision structure and
cross organizational boundaries. Management may be particularly
sensitive to the needs of the organization whereas a technically strong
task force may have a better understanding of the technology and

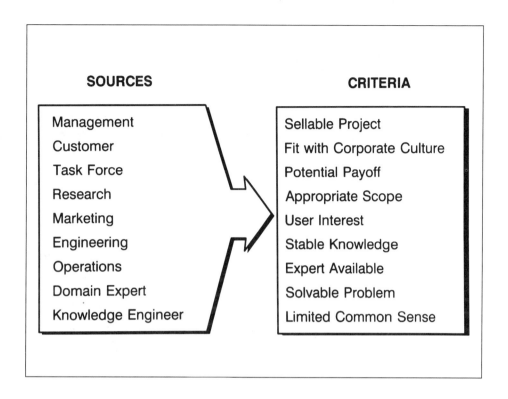

SOURCES

Management
Customer
Task Force
Research
Marketing
Engineering
Operations
Domain Expert
Knowledge Engineer

CRITERIA

Sellable Project
Fit with Corporate Culture
Potential Payoff
Appropriate Scope
User Interest
Stable Knowledge
Expert Available
Solvable Problem
Limited Common Sense

Figure 8.1
Project Selection

where and how it could be most appropriately applied. Additionally, recommendations can be sought from various functional organizations such as marketing or engineering. Members of the team developing the application are also sources of good suggestions. The wise manager will attempt to build an organizational consensus and commitment to the program in advance and maintain this commitment as the program proceeds.

A team of knowledge engineers is not necessarily a good source of project ideas if they are unfamiliar with the specific requirements and functioning of the organization and are unwilling to devote much effort to learn and accept the organizational culture and values. This is particularly true where there are already exaggerated ideas among those who might be affected by the project of the potential displacement of existing human skills from the use of this technology within the organization. Sometimes, the domain experts may be the best source. Since they are likely to be those most directly affected by the use of the new technology, their opinions should be given considerable weight. However, if the domain experts are not well grounded in the capabilities and limitations of AI technology, the knowledge engineers should conduct "seminars" or build simple demonstration systems as examples for communication with domain experts as well as for other interested personnel.

Some bruised egos in either some parts of the organization, or more likely, among members of the AI staff, may be an inevitable result of the project-selection process. However, this should not obscure the fact that unequivocally, the result or product must be saleable to both users and decision makers. The potential beauty of the technology involved is definitely a secondary issue! If the development is intended for external use or incorporation into a product, obviously, the intended customer must feel that it is of value to him or her. If it is an internal project, there may be significant, nontechnical considerations such as company politics. Not being sensitive to these politics can have a devastating effect on the project.

In a large engineering department, there were two design groups we shall designate as Group A and Group B. The output of Group A was required by Group B. Traditionally, Group A had been somewhat lower on the organization chart than Group B, and their work was considered as sort of necessary evil. After some study, it was concluded that some of the expertise of Group A could be incorporated into a knowledge system and made available to Group B in a more easily used fashion. At about this time, Group A was moved up in the organization chart to a level comparable with Group B. This so upset the members of Group B that they refused to use almost anything that came out of Group A.

Providing Group B with a knowledge system whose identified origin was replacement of functions performed by Group A would have been useless. The project would have been doomed to failure no matter how technically successful it was. This project was subsequently abandoned.

In the early days of the interest in the evaluation of AI as a new methodology for use in American industry, a large corporation established an AI research center staffed with academically oriented AI researchers. The initial activities of this group so infuriated the senior line manager of the production arm of the corporation, that all of them were forbidden to enter the plants for which that manager had responsibility.

Another caveat is in order. In selecting a project, try to avoid a "moving target." AI projects must contend with enough uncertainties without having to deal with a fluid knowledge base or frequent changes in the source of the knowledge. These changes may portend difficulties in application definition or management support. If the most desirable project is actually a "moving target" it is sensible to plan to deliver in what amounts to a development environment so that continued changes are easy and do not require extensive translation.

Rather than having a technical emphasis on solution of a problem, the selected project should focus on business requirements. Various rules of thumb have been developed to assist in selecting a good application for a knowledge system (Prerau, 1985). Many of these rules have been developed on the basis of selecting a demonstration project that will be a quick and sure win. There is nothing wrong with such emphasis, but some revision is appropriate for an ROI-oriented evaluation approach. A better strategy may be to focus on a phased approach, in which early results both bound the technical uncertainties and demonstrate value. An important aspect in the present environment, where there have been many stories of the difficulties associated with integration of the final delivery system, is demonstration that integration is feasible. Such a demonstration will, undoubtedly, increase the cost and extend the time of the early phase but it may well save pain and grief later in the program.

A representative, annotated list of the elements of project selection includes:

1. The result of the development of an application is of high and demonstrable value to the organization. The more concrete the benefits can be, the easier it is to justify the ap-

plication. Be prepared to sacrifice technical elegance for utility.

2. The problem is currently solvable (by an expert). There is considerable temptation by those who have read the more optimistic stories about AI to assume that it can do things beyond the capability of a skilled human. Yielding to such temptation is sure disaster! A second point is that the application may not replace the expert but rather perform those tasks that do not require much expertise. There is an interesting and descriptive term for such tasks—no-brainers.

3. An acknowledged expert is available (or can be created). There are several issues here: The expertise may be spread across several individuals; the completed system may so change the nature of the expertise required that it would be necessary for the system design to track changes in the nature of the task and the expertise involved. In this case, the "expertise" is actually developed as the new application is used.

4. The job takes an expert a few minutes to a few hours. This element, as stated, does not suggest the potential for an expert assistant that automates routine or manual tasks, both speeding up the process and freeing the expert to focus on more difficult tasks that cannot be automated. Perhaps, the AI *aficionado* might not feel that such a system was actually "AI." But if the result of using AI technology in a situation like this is beneficial, who cares.

5. There is a large discrepancy between the best and the average performers. This element certainly does not apply in the case of the "no brainer."

6. The amount of common sense utilized is minimal. There are at least two different types of "common sense," one capturable, one not. If the "common sense" is actually private knowledge (see Chapter 7), it may be capturable. If, on the other hand, the decision space is large and "common sense" consists of developing a new strategy and extrapolating from existing knowledge in each new situation, the knowl-

edge is not likely to be captured in any useful form. An expert-assistant strategy is indicated.

7. The rules or procedures for solving the problem can be stated explicitly. This may not be the case if private or shared knowledge is involved.

8. Decisions may have to be made under pressure. No comment here.

9. The answer is not obvious. This sounds like a rule for a winning demonstration only. If it makes money, who cares if it is obvious?

If the application requirements can be met with the use of conventional computing techniques, they should be used because it is probably easier to use conventional methods than the technology of artificial intelligence. However, if it is difficult to define quantitatively and in straightforward serial logic the permutations and approaches to solving the problem, then AI technology is likely to be the better choice.

Some have suggested that AI projects focus on high-value applications. "Pick a problem whose solution could save the organization a couple of million dollars a year." This, of course, dramatically simplifies the issue of being able to show a good return on investment, but how many multi-million dollar opportunities can be identified in the organization? A project of this magnitude may also violate such other constraints as acceptable degree of risk or availability of resources. Other AI developers have concluded that it is better to concentrate on small systems that save perhaps $100,000 per year. Systems of this magnitude are easier to cost-justify, bound the extent of risk, and provide quicker results. It makes sense not to try to hit a home run until you know how to use the bat.

These smaller projects may also have the added benefit of becoming a building block for future projects. Sometimes, the first project will be of limited long-term value, but can be a good basis for a more permanent project. Note, however, that a knowledge system whose product lifetime will be short can also be useful. An example is a system which facilitates introduction of a new product to the field sales force.

When initially getting started with this technology, the risk can be decreased by concentrating on simpler problems. Representative examples are those entailing classification and diagnosis. Another way to bound the risk is to concentrate on areas in which the necessary knowledge is already available in a convenient form. Systems based on published information, for example, rather than on the interviewing of domain experts, facilitate the knowledge-eliciting process. They are also easier to validate. A drawback to these types of systems, however, is that the logic process implemented may be less acceptable to the expert or end user since it most likely does not follow the strategy actually employed. Such systems can also be inflexible.

There are numerous possibilities for increasing the effectiveness of an organization's functions. These might include situations where:

1. Some person or group never seems to get the "word."

2. Things continually "fall through the cracks."

3. Somebody always seems to forget something.

4. There appears to be much duplication of effort.

5. An expert has difficulty in quantifying his or her knowledge.

6. Numerous and expensive mistakes are made which could be reduced by the use of a knowledge system.

Although some of these applications entail carefully walking through the thickets of internal politics, the rewards can justify the effort. Whatever the parameters used in selecting an application, the bottom-line questions should always be asked. What will be the impact on the business? This is of primary importance. How will the proposed project affect the goals of the organization—will it, for example, lead to greater customer satisfaction, enhanced products, or more efficient internal operations? These are probably the overriding criteria.

An experienced technical manager, after much study, carefully selected an initial AI application from a promising group of possibilities. The manager's organization's business was based on sophisticated use of large computer systems. The technical manager felt that a large payoff would result from incorporating AI technology into these large systems. However, in order to limit the risk and development cost, a small subset of the system was selected for the first AI project. Unfortunately, the project was eventually vetoed by a nontechnical financial executive on the grounds that even if the project was successful, it would have no effect on the company's business. In this environment, the technical manager's project selection had placed too much emphasis on development factors and not enough on business implications.

CORPORATE CULTURE

A not-so-subtle factor bearing strongly upon the potential for the success of a project is the nature of corporate culture. Are there some procedures (perhaps unwritten) which, if followed, result in greater cooperation or facilitate getting the job done? Are there prevalent attitudes on the assignment of responsibilities and decentralized decision authority? What is the tolerance level for mistakes? This will affect the degree of conservatism which should be included in the project goals.

Departments within an organization also have different cultures. Contrast the atmosphere and how work is done in marketing, engineering, and manufacturing. Note also the differences in the reward structure. A particular problem that may slow the decision process is caused by a nonstandard procedure. If an AI project cuts across organizational boundaries in a new way, no one may want to risk making a decision.

A champion identified a new application in a corporation that supported a change in procedure that had already been established on a temporary basis. All involved were quite enthusiastic. Unfortunately, the project was long delayed and ultimately dropped because no senior decision maker was willing to take the requisite responsibility.

The process by which technology is introduced is influenced by the organization's culture. Many companies, particularly those with a long history of incorporating new technology, have a central research facility. Such facilities, in addition to performing research, may also be charged with developing initial applications utilizing new technology. These applications are intended to be spread throughout the various operating entities. In some cases, the central facility is staffed and managed at corporate level. In other arrangements, personnel are brought in from the operating entities to participate in development activities appropriate to their own requirements. This has worked well in many situations.

There are other examples in which there is a great deal of antipathy on the part of the operating entities towards almost anything that emanates from the central development facility. Sometimes this antipathy is based on the funding requirements and at other times there may be personalities involved or a feeling that "the central facility just doesn't understand our problem." It then becomes encumbent upon the central facility to spend much of their time on selling the new technology to the operating entities. This has been done by providing training at various levels, seminars, or obtaining active participation in the development project by operating personnel. If the central development facility does not take these attitudes into account, no matter how irrational they may appear to be, prospects for success of the development project are considerably dimmed.

One manager of a central facility struck a deal with one of the operating divisions. He offered to assume most of the initial cost of development of an application of interest to the division if it would provide minimal support the first year and increase the contribution if results were as expected. In this way he obtained both commitment and visible evidence of support for the application development.

Other large organizations, particularly those with diverse business interests, do not have a central development facility. Such facilities are opposed by managers at both the headquarters level and the operating-facility level. How, then, should a new technology be brought into such an organization? Primary concerns of the operating facilities have a shorter time span. Their reward mechanism may be such as to mitigate against investments that have long-term payoffs. A development project using AI technology must thus address these short-term concerns even if they do not appear to be in the long-term interest of the organization. Again, swimming against the tide dims the prospects for the project's success. The case study described in Chapter 14 illustrates the approach that was effective in a large diversified corporation.

Other corporate culture considerations which could influence project success include:

- What is the attitude towards investing in development projects?

- What is the attitude towards utilizing new and perhaps unproven technology?

- What is the attitude of the intended users towards being provided with a knowledge system, perhaps by sources that they feel do not truly understand their needs?

- Have some previous and comparable development projects "bombed"?

- Would the proposed project be considered by peers and management as being in the mainstream interest of the organization?

- Is there a pervasive attitude that too many of the organization's problems are already being caused by computer-based systems?

- Would there be a strong and adverse reaction to organizational changes that might be required by a pervasive AI application?

Sometimes previous activities in AI may have left an imprint.

One large corporation, in the early days of AI, hired an "AI Guru" in a staff position at corporate headquarters, reporting to the president. This individual proved to be insensitive to corporate culture and managed to antagonize most of the division heads by preaching the AI gospel without regard to corporate realities of budget and responsibility. The activity of this individual who departed, unlamented, after several years, left a residue of feeling that made it difficult for any corporate AI champions to suggest new AI projects.

Serious problems may be encountered if a knowledge system is introduced which crosses too many organizational boundaries.

A knowledge system was developed which offered promise for more efficiently moving work through several departments. However, in order to make the system work, established interfaces between the departments would have required modification. The resulting protests finally required the system implementers to segment the system to fit organizational "realities."

Even in a high-tech oriented company, resistance to technical change can be encountered—"the comfort level is disturbed." Installing the knowledge system into an operating entity may require a transitional phase, particularly for handling situations which do not completely fit with the initial system parameters. For a time, it may be necessary to operate the old and new systems simultaneously. These concerns also raise a caution flag on pushing new technology faster than the structure of an organization or its culture can adapt.

This representative list of culture elements underscores the importance of understanding the goals, procedures, and attitudes of an organization: AI technology must be introduced recognizing these factors. Being oblivious to them decreases the likelihood that the knowledge system, in spite of its technical achievements, would be widely construed as a success.

RECEPTIVE ENVIRONMENT

Related to the need for matching the corporate culture is the necessity for having a receptive environment for a project based on AI technology. In addition to the obvious importance of management support, developers and intended users must also become enthusiastic, or at least not antagonistic.

During a tour of a heavy manufacturing facility, an AI development group was studying the feasibility of incorporating knowledge systems into the factory. At one point, they came across an old-time machinist who was operating a large metal-cutting machine equipped with extensive computer controls. However, the machinist was not using the computer controls at all; he even ignored the CRT display. Rather, he would look at the work piece, grunt and then turn a manual crank. After observing the effect of this mechanical crank, he would then again grunt and turn a second crank. This went on for a while, and at no time did this old-time machinist bother with the computer controls. Finally, one of the AI development group members had the temerity to ask, "Why don't you use the computer controls instead of turning those cranks by hand?" The machinist looked down from his platform with disdain and responded, "Look, I am 62 years old. I'll be damned if I'm going to risk my retirement on that computer junk!" After recovering from the bluntness of the machinist's reply, the AI developers decided that this, indeed, would not be a receptive environment for a knowledge system. Much time and expense would have been wasted on developing a knowledge system for this part of the factory. It would have only gathered dust and probably created even more animosity.

There are other examples of inadequate attention having been paid to the idiosyncrasies of the intended user environment.

A knowledge system was developed to assist dealers in selling cars. The value of such a system seemed very great; it would provide the salespeople with a broader range of information which should have been helpful in increasing their commissions. However, it did not work out that way; the salespeople just did not like using the system. Their attitude was that the system reduced personal contact with their sales prospects to an unacceptable level. They were so accustomed to their normal approach to selling cars that any computerized system would, for them, be too impersonal and detract from sales.

Bottlenecks in the organization's flow of work are frequently a good place to look for potential applications of knowledge systems. This is particularly true when the bottlenecks are usually resolved heuristically; that is, by human use of rules of thumb or intuitive understanding of the various pressure points.

As part of their regular duties, employees occasionally had to tediously fill out detailed forms. A knowledge system which eliminated most of the routine work was enthusiastically incorporated by the employees. It was particularly appreciated when the system also accommodated infrequently used forms.

However, if the problems are the result of frequent adverse interaction between organizational entities or between individuals, the knowledge system probably would not be of much help. Further, the champion for the project might get bloodied in the process.

WHAT IS THE SYSTEM INTENDED TO DO?

Although it may seem a truism, it is important always to keep in mind just what the system is supposed to do for a user. Will it be used internally to improve the organization's procedures or activities, or will it be used externally, perhaps incorporated in a product? When considering alternatives for project selection, the intended environment will have an effect. For example, who will really use the system and what will be the atmosphere for its use? It may not be the developers of the system at all, but rather a non-expert with interests different from those of the development engineers. Often, knowledge systems are intended to provide support to personnel with lower skill levels. The purpose is not to replace humans but, instead, to enhance their productivity. This may entail considerable effort in learning the conditions and culture of the user's environment. Also, much of the development task is in designing an effective input-output interface with the user. These efforts may require a substantial investment of time and cost. The magnitude of such an investment and its payback should, of course, influence project selection.

As an example of why the intended user environment must be well understood, consider the design of a knowledge system workstation intended for an office environment (Naffah *et al.*, 1986). Elements of the user environment with which such a knowledge system must contend include:

1. The source of information regarding the task status, the past history of work on the task and the plan for completing it.

2. The appropriate employees to which requests for action should be sent.

3. Who will require notification of deadlines; who needs to be reminded?

4. What supervisor should be called upon when problems arise?

5. Would it be acceptable for the knowledge system to do most of the monitoring of a plan's execution and suggest alternatives?

Note in the above very cursory list, how many factors of the user environment must be well understood in order to have a successful project.

Project selection should also take into account what will happen to the system after it has been delivered to the user. A fielded system might eventually be used in ways far different from those originally conceived by the designers. Such an eventual transition could be a positive aspect of the project. However, preparing for such eventualities entails some up-front development costs. This is another aspect of project selection.

DEFINING THE SCOPE OF THE PROJECT

A final consideration in project selection is determination of the appropriate size of the project. It must be matched with available resources. Will there be enough time, money, people, or development equipment? What would be the attitude of the domain experts? If favorable, would they be able to devote the effort the project would require of them? Predicting the availability of required resources realistically is an important aspect of project selection.

An attraction of AI technology is its effectiveness in solving problems which contain uncertainty, ambiguity, or complexity. However, it is still necessary to put some bounds on these factors in order to have a successful project. If the bounds cannot be determined accurately, particularly for early AI projects, a different application should be considered. The same comment applies to applications where the knowledge base may be incomplete. In such applications would a partial solution be useful or acceptable? On the other hand, it is tempting to incorporate too much knowledge in the system. Even though addition of knowledge increases the performance of the system, potential problems with redundancies and inefficiencies could be encountered (Schaeffer and Marsland, 1985). Either of these circumstances would substantially increase the scope and cost of the project.

As noted previously, there are many good applications of AI technology which do not have the goal of replacing the human experts. Rather, the intent is to assist the experts to do a better job or to improve their work environment. Limiting, at least initially, the extent of assistance to the user, enables a more accurate estimate of project size. Another aid to limiting the scope of a system is to prescribe the range of problems which it is intended to solve. For example, a diagnostic system could be designed to handle the 20 percent of the potential faults that cause 80 percent of the problems.

9

Selling the Project

WHO NEEDS TO BE SOLD?

Exploratory investigations of artificial intelligence technology have been supported by many organizations. Making the transition to applied development usually entails the commitment of greater resources and a change in the supporting organization. This commitment inevitably requires reselling of the project. Because the project is likely to affect many elements of the organization, a multifaceted selling approach is frequently required, as shown in Figure 9.1. Various levels of management must be convinced of the desirability of committing not only dollars but also scarce resources to a program which is different in scale and nature from previously introduced technology. The program may be of such a magnitude or have so many ramifications that high-level management must first be sold. Even if the decision-making authority is delegated to other levels of management, the selling job may be no less difficult.

Chapter 5 noted the changes that are taking place in the AI market. In particular, there is an accelerating change in emphasis from investigation of a new technology to using AI in specific applications.

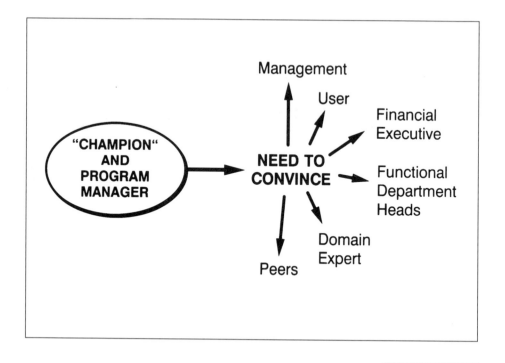

Figure 9.1
Who Must Be Sold on the Project?

Although many organizations are still evaluating AI, an increasing number are oriented toward solutions rather than technology. The approach to selling an AI project must be in consonance with the organization's orientation. Some of the organizational elements who must be sold are the same as for other development programs. These include managers, users, and domain experts. However, there is a difference in emphasis when justifying a technology-exploration project and one intended to solve a particular problem or product requirement.

Previous sections have discussed the importance of having one or more of the intended users involved in development of the project. These intended users must also be sold on the value of the project to them. Few managers are willing to commit resources to develop a product when the intended users say that they are not interested in it. If the intended user is not an individual or a small group of individuals, then a market analysis may be required to project that the product will have a favorable reception.

Other groups within the organization must also be sold on participating in the program, or at least supplying necessary resources. The "owner" of particular resources must be willing to commit these resources to the project. This individual may, for example, be the department manager of the software group which will be required to do some of the programming. It may be the person who controls the hardware or software that will be used. This, again, can be a difficult selling job since the "owner" of these resources may see other uses of the resources which would appear to have a more direct or immediate payoff than the proposed project. Even if the software department manager approves the use of departmental personnel, the software technical people must become enthusiastic contributors. They must be convinced that the project provides an expansion of their technical skills, is useful in their career path, and will be an interesting program to work on. Finally, the domain experts must also be sold. As noted before, they must be convinced that the project does not represent a threat to their livelihood but, rather, will provide an increase in their value to the organization.

HURDLES

Numerous obstacles may appear in the way of a manager who is intent on getting the go-ahead for an AI development project. If the rationale underlying these obstacles is understood, the benefits of this technology can provide a good basis for overcoming them. Among the hurdles which might be encountered are the following:

- Lack of understanding of the technology and its potential benefits
- Management ambivalence
- Size of the investment
- Quantifying ROI
- Resource requirements—time, people, equipment
- Entrenched ideas
- Current delivery vehicle limitations

Although awareness of artificial intelligence technology is now widespread, there are still many misunderstandings about the capabilities and problems of the technology and its implementation. One reaction might be to "leave all that psychology business to the universities, we're in the nuts and bolts business." A reaction at the other extreme might be that "there's really nothing new in that technology. We've been doing that same kind of thing with decision trees and simulations for years." A more moderate position might be taken by a manager who is interested but uncertain about investing in such a project because of her negative reaction to the excessive amount of hyperbole that has been generated about this technology. This manager is inclined to think that the claims seem so extravagant that a "watchful waiting" policy is appropriate until fact and fancy can be more clearly separated.

Presentation of realistic time and cost estimates for completing an operational system may also raise serious concerns in the mind of a manager. The investment required may be substantial, particularly when compared to what has been entailed in developing products or services more familiar to the manager. The manager asks:

1. "What is the likelihood that the estimates are inaccuarate and that the project may end up costing considerably more?"

2. "With these nagging doubts in mind, why not select a safer project?"

3. "It certainly will be easier to quantify the return on investment on a safer project."

4. "The AI project has many intangibles, and even though results look promising, how can you quantify them in terms of conventional ROI approaches?"

This inability to quantify the ROI creates problems not only in dealing with decision makers, but also other organizations which may influence the final decisions. There may well be established policies which say that no project will be approved which cannot indicate a payback within a certain number of months.

Objections to initiating an AI program do not always have a logical basis—at least as viewed by the individual trying to sell the program.

At one company there was a large data-processing organi-zation which had a lot of "clout" with top management. Practi-cally all the hardware had been supplied by one computer manufacturer. This hardware was not really a good choice for any of the AI projects suggested by the technical manager. The data-processing group, claiming that it was uneconomic to support other manufacturers' hardware, succeeded in derailing the AI project.

Perhaps the only way to sell a project at this company would have been to trade development efficiency for expediency.

Another hurdle is the need for scarce resources during the development, installation, and maintenance of the AI-based product. Once the difficult problem of allocating personnel with the appropriate skills to the project has been settled, specialized hardware and software is needed to obtain an efficient development environment. Some have claimed that AI technical development people should be given whatever equipment they want, regardless of its cost. They claim that the improvement, efficiency and eventual benefits of a well-executed project are so great that concern about the cost of developmental hardware and software is shortsightedness. Most employees of industrial organizations react bitterly to such a statement, feeling it to be totally unrealistic. However, as long as the demand for skilled AI system builders remains high, the provision of advanced development hardware may be an important recruiting tool.

Typically, there is a well-established procedure for acquiring capital equipment, and invariably there are more requests for purchasing capital equipment than there are funds available. Priorities must be set as to which capital equipment will be purchased. These decisions can be very difficult. A manufacturing engineer states, "If you let me purchase this component-insertion machine for $100,000, it would save ten minutes per printed circuit board assembly time. This would translate into a payback period of 13.5 months." Contrast this with a development engineer who states, "I need to purchase this specialized computer for $100,000. My development environment will thus be made much more efficient, but I cannot quantify how many man-months I will save in the process." This presents a difficult problem for the decision maker with responsibility for the purchase of capital equipment, as well as the development engineer.

Another possible hurdle is represented by entrenched ideas. In the middle of a presentation on the benefits of AI technology, an old-time programmer sitting at the back of the room interjects, "Hey, what's so great about this technology? I've been doing the same thing with FORTRAN for 20 years!" It may, indeed, be possible to devise a problem solution implemented in FORTRAN. It then becomes an uphill battle to convince this qualified and experienced programmer that AI technology would provide a better solution.

Resistance may also appear as reluctance to change procedures which appear to have been satisfactory for a long time. The vernacular maxim "If it ain't broke, don't fix it" cannot be dismissed lightly. Resistance may also exist among those who perceive the project as a threat, as has been noted previously. Even if the project is not seen as a serious threat, fear or doubt about a new technology may be an obstacle. For example, some manufacturing managers may have but a limited perception of either the capability or limits of a factory-oriented knowledge system. They would probably be uncertain about a new technology until they had gained some confidence in it, perhaps from demonstrations in a related application.

Legitimate concerns can exist with regard to the currently available delivery vehicles. It is one thing to invest $100,000 in hardware to develop an AI product; it is quite another to consider putting 20 or 50 of these $100,000 machines on the factory floor. Similarly, is it feasible to put an expensive and specialized machine and software into thousands of desktop terminals or a military environment? The issue of delivery vehicles is discussed in Chapter 13.

An interesting survey was conducted on the major barriers to the development and use of knowledge systems (Fried, 1986). The primary barriers noted in the survey were:

1. Lack of knowledge engineers

2. Overall cost of knowledge systems development and application

3. Difficulties in interfacing to existing traditional applications

4. Lack of cooperative, articulate experts

5. Lack of awareness or commitment of potential users

6. Cost of hardware and software

7. Questionable utility or benefit of applications

These barriers are similar to the investment and resource requirement hurdles listed at the beginning of this section.

IMPORTANCE OF A CHAMPION

In order to surmount the hurdles noted in the previous section, it is important to have a dedicated champion. This person should be committed to exploiting the potential of AI and strongly motivated to convince others in the organization.

If the organization is already sufficiently convinced of AI's potential, the champion should stress other aspects. It may be necessary to more closely conform to established procedures for evaluating development proposals. A more quantitative analysis of a specific project's benefits for internal operations, competitive position, customer responsiveness, etc., may be required. However, even in these circumstances, the status of AI technology is such that support from other elements of the organization will usually be essential. An effective champion must possess an unusual combination of qualities:

1. Technical competence

2. Salesmanship

3. Stature in the organization sufficient to influence decision makers

4. Perseverance

5. Enthusiasm

6. Good understanding of the organization's goals, procedures, and operating environment

7. Willingness to assume personal and career risk in return for possible gain

A member of a progressive development group became convinced of the benefits of AI technology. The development group had a good record of incorporating hardware and software advances into their designs, but only after being convinced by demonstrable advantages. After much discussion, the champion was authorized to develop an initial prototype. After demonstrating the limited-capability prototype, he enthusiastically began generating project plans, marketing strategies, and ideas for other applications. Unfortunately, this flurry of activity was unfocused and eventually triggered adverse management reaction. The champion had enthusiasm and perseverance, but was blocked by his low stature in the organization and confusion about the nature of the organization's goals and operating environment.

Depending upon the hurdles being encountered, an effective champion should employ various strategies. Particularly helpful is to obtain a favorable estimate of the value of a completed project from a potential user whose opinions are respected in the organization. A sponsor is needed in the user organization who would strongly support the project. This sponsor should have adequate authority and be closely associated with the business goals which the proposed system is intended to address. Credibility with management is also greatly enhanced when a department manager agrees, "If you provide me with a knowledge system having those capabilities, I will subtract $50,000 from my annual operating budget."

Another valuable ally is a recognized domain expert. Commitment from an expert about the utility of the project is significant. Also helpful are demonstrations indicating capabilities of the technology. The demonstration could operate on a personal computer using an available software shell which has a particularly impressive user interface. When these demonstrations are provided to various elements or levels of the organizations, they frequently trigger ideas for still other applications which might not even have occurred to the champion.

Even with all of this support, much of the burden of identifying promising AI applications remains on the champion, particularly if the organization has not yet had extensive experience in using the technology in specific projects.

A champion who was directing a promising AI develop-ment project began searching for additional applications. This became increasingly difficult since her position in an R&D group did not provide enough insight into other company activity. In frustration, she exclaimed: "Isn't there somebody near the top of this organization who knows the tough problems we need to solve?"

People "at the top" are likely to be well aware of many of the tough problems, but the channel of communication to the AI champion is not a direct one. One cannot assume ready access to a font of knowledge on all the problems amenable to solution by AI technology.

UNDERSTANDING MOTIVATIONS

As in most marketing situations, it is essential to understand the motivation of the person who will grant approval for implementing the project. Are there prevalent attitudes: "Don't muddy the waters" or "We can't afford to have moss growing around here." What benefit will this project provide for the decision maker, as well as for the organization?

Is anyone being subjected to strong pressure to reduce the costs in a particular operation? Dealing with such factors may be distasteful to a dedicated manager, but without satisfactory responses, the project can stall.

An AI proponent in a central research facility was having difficulty in persuading operational division personnel to take a serious interest in this new technology. Their reaction was: "Why should we commit resources to this untried technology? Our business position is secure." Near the central research facility was the headquarters of a large company in a related business. This company was suffering serious erosion of their market. The AI proponent was finally able to get the attention of the operating

> *division personnel by telling them: "Look across the street at the XYZ company. See what is happening to them and their employees as a result of not investing in new technology."*

When identifying these motivations, it should be remembered that the intended user of the product and the person who funds the project may have different goals. Both sets of goals may be valid but some may be in conflict. The funder of the project may wish to reduce labor costs; the intended user may be more concerned with job security.

Management motivations may also differ. The primary orientation of upper-level corporate management is generally not technical curiosity but, rather, the addition of value to the enterprise by the optimum allocation of available resources. Priority decisions must be made, some of which are for short-term result. Some managers are particularly sensitive about approving projects bearing any resemblance to previous failure or bad experience. Managers also make decisions in the context of their current operating environment. Even if an application has good prospects for increasing productivity in a factory, it will not be enthusiastically received by a management already concerned that the factory is operating at only half of capacity.

One possible scenario might be posed by a cautious but interested manager: "I will provide you with $25,000 over a two-month period. Now, what can you show me about the potential of AI within that constraint?" After sufficient study, the champion could respond, "We could build a limited-capability prototype with that money and timetable. It would demonstrate the feasibility of the technology for helping to solve the problem that has been nagging us on production. It would then take another $750,000, and 14 months, to put a working system on the factory floor."

10

Who Designs
the System?

During initial consideration of an artificial intelligence system, an important decision is the assignment of design responsibility. Who will specify the system parameters; who will elicit the knowledge; who will develop the software? The assignment of responsibility should be influenced by several factors:

1. The extent of in-house design development and maintenance competence

2. Time and cost trade-offs

3. Available, qualified manpower

4. Proprietary concerns

5. Marketing considerations

Obviously, if the organization does not have extensive experience in designing and building sophisticated software systems, or if adequately skilled personnel are not available, then the design responsibility must be placed elsewhere. Evaluation of the requirements for maintenance and the source for it during the life of the software is of equal importance. Maintaining any software program can be an involved and expensive process and initial experience with large AI software systems, particularly in a delivery environment, show a trend to high cost. Involvement in the development process is probably the best training for a maintenance group. Thus the requirement for building a reliable and low-cost maintenance capability should be factored into the assignment decision. Experience is an important part of the ability to provide reliable maintenance. One successful approach has been a team effort, where the in-house maintenance group is trained by participation in the design and building phase. Time and cost trade-offs are unique to the particular situation, and at times, the correct approach is not obvious.

Even if an organization has only limited experience in developing such systems, it may choose to retain the design in-house to alleviate concerns on releasing sensitive proprietary information. Market considerations that should influence the decision include: requirements for product distinction, in-house design credibility, strategic business relationships, and availability of external support.

PURCHASING A COMPLETE SYSTEM

An alternative to in-house development is purchase of a packaged system from a company specializing in AI products. Such a system may be custom-designed or one for which there is broader market potential. Considerations relating to the selection of a supplier for such a system include:

1. Financial stability of the supplier.

2. Nature, quality and cost of customer support offered by the supplier. Such support can prove to be a considerable cost item.

3. Product capability.

4. Applicability of the product for its intended use.

5. Ease of modification and maintenance of the product.

6. Capability for control of proprietary information.

7. Reliability and documentation.

8. Training.

Since there are so many new companies in the AI business, it is important to verify the track record of the proposed supplier. This may be difficult if the supplier has but a few customers; still, if possible, contact should be made with the customers to determine their experiences with this supplier. If the AI system has already been designed and is offered as a complete system, it may either have features beyond those required by the intended user, or satisfy only a narrow spectrum of the intended user's needs. Furthermore, the supplier may be reluctant to invest in modifying the product for only one customer. The importance of customer support should not be underestimated. Both technical progress and changing knowledge bases make it mandatory that the supplier provide necessary support or that the product be designed for maintenance and upgrading by the customer or user. Consequently, the supplier must be able to provide adequate training in both using and maintaining the system.

Many of the considerations relating to purchasing of a packaged system are also relevant to obtaining a software development shell (use of these software tools is discussed in Chapter 13). Particularly important as a basis for selection are customer support, flexibility, and product features. There are other factors relevant to a make-or-buy decision on a development shell; a controversial issue is access to the shell's source code. This code may be needed for a better understanding of how the system works, to permit modification during development, to achieve a more efficient fielded system, or for delivery to a customer. Acquiring the source code raises issues of proprietary information, licensing fees, multiple use, and incorporation with other products and services (Warn, 1986).

WORKING WITH CONSULTANTS

Many consulting organizations and individuals have a high degree of competence in specifying and designing knowledge systems. Unfortunately, however, there are many more consultants whose capabilities fall far short of claims. Various arrangements can be worked out with consultants. Some prefer to take total responsibility for the project. They will participate in selecting the project, elicit the knowledge, then design and test the complete system. Their preference may be to take an assignment for a single large and complex system rather than a number of smaller systems. An organization might select such a consulting arrangement if it feels there would be little need for developing additional systems or if it feels that the time and expense of developing in-house competence is not warranted.

Another approach is to have the consultant only support the development of a knowledge system rather than take full responsibility. The consultant participates in selecting and specifying the system and, perhaps, carries the responsibility for the initial prototype. During this early phase, the consultant might also provide training for the organization's own development personnel. Subsequent to acceptance of the prototype, further arrangements would be made allocating responsibilities for the balance of the project. A disadvantage of this approach is that development time and cost would probably be somewhat greater since the consultant must take time out to train the organization's personnel. An obvious benefit, however, is that the organization eventually acquires in-house competence.

There are a number of trade-offs in working with consultants. The cost of consultants can be quite high, but this must be balanced against the cost and time in developing in-house competence. Good consulting organizations may have a broader range of experience than that available in-house. They may have better access to skilled personnel and, significantly, be better able to retain the services of these skilled people since they can offer a challenging range of assignments. Consultants may also be more objective about the organization's requirements or problems as well as the market potential or user interest for such a system. (There is possibility of a conflict of interest here.) A disadvantage arises if the consultant does not know much about the organization's procedures and business environment. The organization would, therefore, be paying to educate the consultant in the specifics of its own operation. Some destructive antagonisms may also develop. If reliance is placed upon the consultant for a complete package, in-house personnel will gain only limited experience in adapting the package to the organization's infrastructure.

Several measures should be taken to improve the probability of having a successful project. Initially, of course, the consultant's competence in developing the type of system required should be evaluated. Secondly, a careful understanding of the responsibilities of both the organization and the consultant should be worked out. There may be many unknowns which complicate the writing of an appropriate work statement for an AI system. Provision should be included in the work statement for further definition as work proceeds and more information is obtained. The work statement should cover such other matters as the extent of training to be provided; requirements for accessibility of domain experts; acceptance criteria for both prototype and complete system; provision for maintenance. Finally, costs and schedules must be defined, although there should be sufficient flexibility to accommodate the uncertainties in this type of project. Contractual stipulations should cover such matters as eventual ownership and marketing rights for the system, protection of proprietary information, and competitive constraints.

SUPPORT FROM ACADEMIC INSTITUTIONS

Establishing good relations with academic institutions can be helpful. In addition to the desirability of supporting students and professors, organizations may derive great benefit from access to current research at these institutions. Academic institutions can also be a valuable source of information and an eventual source of skilled personnel. There is, however, a considerable difference in results that may be obtained from assigning major system design and development responsibilities to academic institutions as opposed to consultants.

Among the advantages that may be obtained from working with academic institutions are:

1. Easy and fast access to important research developments

2. Knowledgeable professors and students to work on the project

3. Enthusiasm and creativity

4. Information about what other organizations are doing in related fields

5. Objectivity, particularly with reference to evaluation of hardware and software capabilities

Difficulties which may be encountered include:

1. Different motivation between academic institutions and industrial organizations

2. Problems in reliable scheduling of student work on the project

3. Maintaining control of proprietary information in an academic environment

4. Probable minimal attention to documentation and maintenance

5. Possible antagonism between research-oriented personnel and profit-oriented organizations

6. Lackadaisical attitudes about meeting schedule and cost commitments

7. Relegation of the project to second-string status if more interesting developments or other sponsors appear

In spite of these potential difficulties, there have been successful collaborations between academic institutions and industrial organizations in the development and application of AI technology. Certainly, industrial support of academic research is a vital concern but commercial enterprises cannot afford to be overly altruistic. A key to working effectively with academic institutions is selection of applications closely attuned to their research interests. If at all possible, the institutions should be allowed flexibility in scheduling, particularly if extensive research is required. The emphasis, therefore, should be primarily on technology transfer rather than in meeting the specific goals and constraints of a commercial project.

STRATEGIC BUSINESS RELATIONSHIPS

Recently, there has been an increase in relationships between AI suppliers and organizations intending to implement knowledge systems. Several large corporations have taken equity positions in small or start-up AI systems companies. The intent is to maintain the entrepreneurial spirit of the smaller AI company while still providing the large company with preferred access to the technology. There is also an implied or contractual commitment from the AI company to pay particular attention to the needs of the large corporation. The price paid for the equity investment may appear disproportionate to the level of current earnings. This is not a strong deterrent for a major corporation. A primary motivation for such action is the desire to stay at the forefront of a technology which may be important in the corporation's future.

A number of third-party and value-added arrangements have been established. Typically, a supplier of specialized AI hardware and software will provide technology to another company which has a favorable market position. Presumably, it is advantageous to both organizations. One organization benefits by having market exposure which it could not conveniently obtain on its own; the other obtains a product which would be too expensive or impractical to develop with its own resources. From the standpoint of a user organization, these third-party arrangements can be quite acceptable, provided that there are satisfactory arrangements for training in maintenance and support of the product.

There have also been success stories in establishing strategic links between customer and supplier. In these arrangements, the supplier provides the user or customer with hardware, software or development support. There are several motivations for these arrangements. The customer may be prominent in a major market of interest to the supplier, and completing a successful project for such a customer would be advantageous to the AI supplier. The customer may also eventually market the system into niches which would otherwise be less accessible to the AI supplier. Entering into such arrangements can be beneficial to both organizations but establishing the benefits and agreeing on them can be difficult and time consuming. Other potential problems with these arrangements include conflicting priorities and allocating costs for development.

A relatively recent participant in the structure of the computer industry is the value-added reseller (VAR). Typically, the VAR will purchase hardware or software from an existing supplier, incorporate additional features, and sell the combined product into a particular market segment. Competent VARs may have better knowledge of the market segment and its requirements than the primary supplier of the hardware and software. They may also be better able to support the investment in resources required to reach a specialized market. With regard to knowledge systems, VARs could be considered as a supplier with an essentially "off the shelf" system for internal applications. For external applications, they could be considered as an adjunct of a company's own marketing organization, with responsibility for adapting a generalized system within the parameters of a particular market segment. Marketing activities might also be aided by contracting with an independent software company to validate the performance of a knowledge system.

DEFENSE CONTRACTING

There are some striking differences between commercial and defense-oriented organizations in the rationale and procedures for implementing AI technology. Much of the funding for AI research has come from government organizations. Defense and space agencies continue to have an active interest in applying AI technology in complex situations. Government contractors have strong incentives for endeavoring to incorporate AI technology into their hardware and software systems.

The perspective for defense contractors and their AI applications is frequently quite different from that of a consumer-oriented organization. For one thing, the time spans are considerably greater. It is not unusual for ten years to elapse between definition of the initial military need and ultimate field deployment. There may also be a wide gap in perception of the project between the initial military contracting agency and the user organization. Also, although the total cost of a military program may be high as compared to commercial programs, severe cost (and schedule) constraints may be placed upon the project development team. Added to this are operational environment factors, compatibility with hardware and software already in the inventory, and long-term training and maintenance requirements. All of this is not meant to imply that building defense systems is impractical but, rather, that there are ununusual design constraints (Akey and Dunkelberger, 1987).

Department of Defense and NASA-supported AI research programs show promising potential for helping to solve difficult problems. These programs may also assist their contractors in defraying some of the costs of acquiring competence and capability in the use of this technology. Some of these research and development programs may eventually provide the technology that will be used in fielded systems. As a result, cost-sharing arrangements for R&D programs between government and contractor are common.

Marketing considerations may be complex. Bidders on many recent government programs must demonstrate a high level of competence in AI technology in order to win the award. For many large organizations, particularly in aerospace, demonstration of competence is not difficult. However, there frequently are specialized areas in which even a large organization can realistically claim only marginal competence. In such circumstances teaming relationships are frequently established; for example, with a much smaller organization that has already developed the technology in specialized applications. The small and large companies then have complementary strengths for winning a contract. There are, however, drawbacks for both organizations in such arrangements. The small organization may not be in a position to undertake a substantial cost-sharing arrangement. There may also be concerns over being enveloped by the large company. Conversely, the large company may be concerned that the smaller specialized company may have grand designs on taking over an ever larger part of the contract's funded tasks. Finally, conflicts may arise over the allocation of responsibilities, costs, schedule commitments, etc.

A common concern for both contractors and government agencies is the issue of data rights. Upon completion of a project, does the government become sole owner of all of the design material, both hardware and software? This may present a serious disadvantage to a small company aspiring to market the output of their work in other niches of the market.

ROLE OF THE DATA-PROCESSING ORGANIZATION

As the use of personal computers (PCs) became more and more widespread, numerous battles over turf broke out. These involved such issues as:

1. Which part of the organization controls the selection and acquisition of these small computers?

2. What procedures must be followed to control access to and the modification of corporate data bases?

3. How should the PCs and their software be networked together?

4. Who is responsible for developing or acquiring new software?

Data processing and management information system (MIS) groups have found it necessary to modify some of their established procedures to deal with the challenges of PC technology. The intent of this modification is to support distributed processing on a network of small computers, while retaining the overall responsibility for insuring that the organization's corporate resources are used most effectively. As AI technology is more widely used, what will be the change in the role of these data processing and MIS groups? Will AI become just another part of data processing (Schindler, 1986)?

Numerous tradeoffs are possible for assigning responsibilities for developing or utilizing AI systems. Should the existing MIS group supervise the development of information systems, or should a new in-house AI group take over that responsibility? Factors to be considered include:

1. The level of interaction needed between these systems and existing corporate data bases

2. Familiarity with the organization's needs, procedures and existing data-processing systems

3. Cost of equipping, training, and motivating a specialized AI staff

4. Built-in NIH biases ("That's not our idea, just do it the same way we always have.")

5. Attitudes towards working closely with "nonprofessional" or "hands-on" experts such as those on the factory floor or in customer service

6. Requirement for new specialties

7. Distinctions between development of systems intended to improve internal operations and development of new products or services

8. The amount of EDP resources required to develop or run an AI application program

The MIS groups certainly have had extensive experience in interfacing with many elements in the organization. However, they have not always been successful in completely understanding the needs of users or the methods used in accomplishing specific tasks. Although they may be familiar with computer technology, some MIS personnel are not suited for the level of innovative development required with the current state of the artificial intelligence art. Conversely, they may have become by reason of previous experience much more realistic about scheduling and cost requirements. Finally, motivations and priorities may favor establishment of a specialized AI group.

One of us spent several hours with the members of a consulting group that specialized in the design of large database systems. The purpose of the meeting was to explore the commonalities and differences between AI and "conventional" data-base system practice. There were two interesting conclusions from the meeting: First, that the AI community was just beginning to learn what the data-processing community had learned long ago, and second, that the major difference was one of focus. The designer of a data-base system must ruthlessly focus on commonality, suppressing any individual differences. The designer of an AI system, on the other hand, gives greatest emphasis to the individual and his or her needs.

As distributed computing power becomes more available, it may be possible to embed individual support systems within the common whole.

IN-HOUSE DEVELOPMENT

Many organizations can justify the investment entailed in establishing semiautonomous AI groups. How should such a group be organized and how can this capability be disseminated into the operating divisions (Kowalik, 1985)? These questions have been faced frequently by central research groups. There are some distinctions, however, in the case of AI technology. This new technology will quite likely affect such things as clerical procedure, in addition to, say, improved processing technology or products which have typically been the focus of a central research group. Transferring AI technology effectively from a research group, therefore, requires working relationships with several types of operating entities. There are various options as to how an in-house AI group should be organized and operated. The following presentation of options is premised on having made the investment decision to staff and train a competent group of AI specialists.

The charter of the AI group might be responsibility for all AI projects. These might include applications to support internal operating procedures, and development of new processes, products and services. This can be an efficient approach since it makes good use of expensive specialized equipment. An enthusiastic and productive environment can be generated by peer interaction and commonality of goals. Also, if funding is secure, developers are not as distracted by concerns about arbitrary reductions-in-force or lay-offs.

Criticism of such an approach typically relates to a buildup of insularity or "ivory tower" outlook. A separate AI group may also have difficulty in generating widespread support from the operating entities in the organization. Part of the problem may come from self-perception of members of the AI group that they constitute an elite. Further, some of the mystique of AI may just be perceived as sloppy work by more conventional computer scientists. Sometimes, arbitrary financial support is required from the operating entities, which further increases the friction. Conflicts can also arise over selection of projects and establishment of priorities. A longer-term problem with this approach may be encountered if an eventual decision is made to integrate the AI design group into the mainstream design and operation functions. The problem is exacerbated if the AI group has been isolated from "the real world." Although this design group might, indeed, comprise talented and uniquely experienced individuals, the perception of them as a management-designated elite might heighten the tension. These potential problems are further reason to maintain close relations, including personnel rotations, with the line organizations.

An opposite approach is to permit every operating entity that needs AI technology to establish its own capability. This is a good fit with a management philosophy which emphasizes decentralized responsibility and authority. These separate AI groups are, presumably, more closely attuned to their organizational component's requirements and priorities. Obvious disadvantages include duplication of effort, higher investment costs, time delays, staffing problems, and overlapping activity with other organizations. Providing "seed money" from corporate headquarters to the operating entities can have a salutary effect. Developers "working within the bowels" of the organization are encouraged by recognition of their efforts at a management level far removed from their own. Also, line managers are more inclined to risk their scarce resources, since even a little seed money indicates that headquarters is interested in the project.

Some diversified companies have set up task forces comprising representatives from the operating divisions as well as corporate functions. Responsibility for implementation decisions and the investment required is retained by the operating division. The advantages of this approach include a good fit with management philosophy, a better understanding of division procedures and requirements, and some initially shared training costs. The task force may also serve as focus for implementation of corporate-wide purchasing agreements and sharing of experiences obtained while building skills and developing AI systems. Disadvantages of this approach include conflicting demands on the team members and the need for each operating entity to make its own investment in developing AI capability. One company's experiences with this approach is described in a case study included in Chapter 14 of this book.

A few large companies have set up extensive centralized facilities for training and the development of prototypes. Such facilities are staffed with small but permanent groups of AI professionals. The staff is then augmented, on a rotating basis, with representatives from the operating organization. These representatives, after having been trained and assisted in developing an initial prototype, subsequently return to their divisions. After the organizational bugs had been smoothed out, this became an efficient approach to technology transfer in a large aerospace company. One of the difficulties encountered was in persuading the operating divisions to send one or more of their skilled personnel to the training center for an extended time (Kowalik, 1986).

Project Organization and Management

SCOPE

This chapter describes the building of an AI system from the viewpoint of a project manager. To a certain extent, the information presented in this chapter overlaps that given in Chapter 7. However, Chapter 7 describes the system-building process in more detail and from the viewpoint of the participant in the process rather than that of the project manager. Because there is value to be obtained from explanation of both viewpoints, we give both.

DISTINCTIVE ASPECTS OF AI DEVELOPMENT PROJECTS

The methodology utilized in developing AI systems differs somewhat from that used in developing other computer-based products. Project leaders whose experience has taught them how to manage conventional software development programs successfully find that they must modify or augment their management techniques. Certainly, some familiar project management controls are still appropriate: schedule and cost milestones, design reviews, design specifications, test planning, etc. There are, however, some phases of an AI development project which are quite different. The knowledge development process requires different disciplines and alternative management approaches as discussed in Chapter 7. Certainly, effective procedures for eliciting the knowledge and representing it are critical to the success of an AI project (Waterman, 1986).

Conventional wisdom on how to develop software systems is not totally applicable to the development of knowledge systems. Sad experience has taught project engineers the necessity of carefully structuring a software development project. In particular, project engineers have learned the importance of specifying, to the greatest degree possible, exactly what the software system is intended to do, prior to any coding. Another essential task is the definition of software modules and interfaces during early phases of the project. There are many horror stories of the dire consequences which occurred when these procedures were not carefully followed. Additionally, design techniques such as top-down and structured program methodology have been instituted in order to better manage the software development and its subsequent maintenance. Conventional software developers emphasize the freezing of specifications and system design prior to starting detailed software coding.

Some of these techniques are applicable to systems utilizing AI technology but others are not. Frequently, AI technology is intended to assist in solving problems which are poorly defined or for which the information needed to solve the problem is incomplete. It is during the course of eliciting the knowledge that the problem becomes better defined or when the available knowledge is augmented. This approach makes it difficult to define the system completely prior to starting design. At times, the top-down approach is effective, but in other circumstances, a bottom-up design is more efficient. Another difference from conventional software design is the ability to rapidly produce a prototype. As noted, many prototypes can be developed in from one to three months. Although a prototype built in this way is likely to be limited in capability, it will be valuable in further characterizing the requirements of the system, the feasibility of the approach, and evaluating the user interface that will be required.

Another important feature of a rapid prototype based on AI methods is the relative ease by which additional information may be added or the existing knowledge base modified. These features of AI technology make it undesirable to insist upon relying only on the same project management techniques that have been effective in developing other types of software systems.

As the design of a knowledge system matures, some of the more conventional software design and management techniques may, indeed, become appropriate. For example, tuning methods may be found which increase the computational efficiency and speed. Such tuning may require knowledge about the problem and its solution. It may even be effective to discard the knowledge manipulation or search techniques that were used in the initial design of the prototype. Conversion to a more conventional algorithmic solution may improve speed, require less processing power or memory. It may also have the added advantage of being easy to code in a more conventional high-order language. This, of course, would have the advantages of greater familiarity and also compatibility with other hardware and software systems. Although the manner in which the system is modified or updated is somewhat different for knowledge systems, there is the same requirement for maintenance and security as with more conventional software systems.

INTEGRATION

Most of the literature about AI has focused on the design of an AI system and not the integration issues associated with the operational use of such a system. There are several sensible reasons for such neglect, although the wise manager should recognize that such neglect can only be temporary in the life of an operational system.

Frequently, the primary focus during the early stages of the development of an AI system is to determine that the technology risk is adequately bounded and that the final system will justify its cost. Under these circumstances, it is best to defer most of the integration activity, beyond demonstration of feasibility, until later when the technical risk of integration is generally less and the potential value of the system can be measured without connecting it to on-line data sources. Deferring a capability for on-line operation till later does not mean that providing on-line operation can be done immediately or is inexpensive. In fact, it is likely that integration of an AI system may involve considerably more effort and cost than has been expended in the development of the original prototype. It may also be that a selected supplier of AI technology has given less attention to integration issues than might be expected and the final integration effort may provide some surprises.

A preliminary evaluation of expected integration issues should be made prior to a major commitment to specific hardware or software or both and a reasonable reserve for cost growth and schedule slip provided.

Another integration issue needs to be considered, the impact of the completed system on the working conditions of the users. This issue, discussed in Chapters 7, 8, and 9, can be of considerable importance in the success of an application.

Project leaders may have to develop still another skill while managing AI development projects. The widespread interest in artificial intelligence increases the likelihood that the project leader will be asked to give interviews to both technical and nontechnical media. This can be either satisfyingly challenging or fraught with problems. Trade-offs must be made between developing good public relations for the organization against disclosing too much of what the organization is doing with this technology. Good reporters are quite capable of extracting more information about a project than competitive circumstances warrant. They are also sometimes prone to exaggerate in order to increase interest in the story.

During the early phases of his company's development of AI technology, a project manager was interviewed by a large-circulation computer journal. The project manager stated that his company had initiated about ten AI development projects. When the story subsequently appeared in the journal it was headlined, "The company has initiated 100 development projects." This tenfold exaggeration (individual project costs were typically a million dollars apiece) caused much irritation and embarrassment to the company and damaged its credibility with potential customers.

The project leader or organization spokesperson must develop the ability to explain subjects which are highly technical or complex in a manner which can be understood by individuals with less background in this technology. They must also be able to extrapolate to other applications of the technology, but again, within the bounds of good company practice.

PROJECT PLANNING

Many elements of project plans that are used in other engineering development programs are also applicable to systems using AI technology. Major elements are diagrammed in Figure 11.1 and

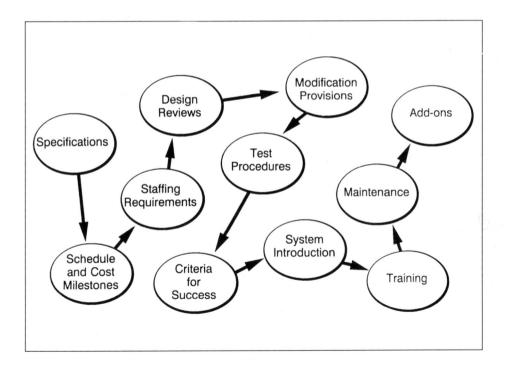

Figure 11.1
Elements of Project Plans

subsequently discussed. For clarity, the figure depicts these elements as occurring serially in a generalized time sequence. For more complex project plans, there may be considerable overlap or recursion.

Careful planning is a prerequisite for a successful AI project. But what is meant by a successful project? There may be numerous uncertainties and ill-defined aspects of a problem to which this technology will be applied. It then becomes difficult to determine whether or not the project is actually successful. An important element in project success is having goals which are clearly understood by the developers and management. For example, is the primary intent to learn the technology or to solve a specific problem?

In order to avoid misunderstandings and setbacks to other applications of this technology, the project plan should include clear and agreed-upon criteria for success. These criteria should be understood by all concerned parties. They should take into account user needs as well as any constraints placed upon the developers. As the project evolves and more is understood about the application, some of the criteria can be modified.

Examples of criteria that might be used to define success are that the system:

1. Solve representative problems satisfactorily.

2. Increase the effectiveness of the user in a demonstrable way.

3. Provide recognizable product enhancement or features.

4. Respond to a market opportunity or pressure in a specific manner.

5. Satisfy the "check-signer." (This may be the most important but most difficult to define in advance.)

To the extent possible, the criteria should be made specific. For example, what new product features would be achieved by using this technology? Or, what would the specific market opportunity be and how would this project assist in satisfying it? Designating a representative problem for a diagnostic system may be relatively easy, but selecting an appropriate problem for a system that is intended to be an intelligent assistant to a design expert may be much more difficult to do in advance.

One source of failure to meet success criteria is inadequate definition of the scope of the problem during the project planning cycle. As described in Chapter 9, defining the scope is very important for selling the project, but is equally important in implementing it. Other potential problems include integration of various knowledge sources with the system and the complexities of technology transfer.

Difficulties may be encountered in transferring responsibility for maintaining a knowledge system from the development group to the users. The users should be brought into the project early enough for them to become familiar with the system, its capabilities, and its limitations. This involvement can be costly and time consuming and, therefore, should be part of the initial project planning. If the application entails providing assistance to a human expert, the user should not be expected to immediately abandon the present way of doing things. A more practical approach is to continue existing methods while concurrently introducing the new knowledge system. A phased introduction helps build user confidence, as well as lessening the impact of modifications and retraction of features. This phased operation provides a mechanism for transition as well as training and, importantly, an evaluation of how much improvement is provided by the new knowledge system.

Another aspect of technology transfer may be the need to incorporate additional changes and capabilities in working procedures when introducing knowledge systems. An AI control system, for example, may permit human intervention, but these interventions must be promptly reported and recorded so that the system contains a current representation of process status.

Task definition is an important part of project planning. In addition to defining system parameters, the role of the various participants in the development and application phases of the project should be spelled out. This will reduce misunderstandings between managers, developers, and users, as well as keeping expectations within reasonable bounds. Preparing a detailed design specification may be initially difficult for some applications, but remember that this specification need not be set in concrete. As more is learned about the problem and its solution, the design specifications can be continually refined. As far as the participants are concerned, the project plan should indicate the individual responsibilities of developers and users as well as their relationships. Care should be taken to define who is really going to use the system and the background of the user.

If, during the project planning phase, the problem solution appears to be growing too large or intractable, segmentation into smaller problems should be considered. Segmentation of large problems into smaller ones is influenced by several factors:

1. Magnitude of the development problem

2. Resources available (including trained personnel)

3. Time and cost constraints

4. Sub-problem priorities

5. Internal "selling" considerations

6. Poorly defined knowledge base

7. Maintenance considerations

As in other development projects, demonstrable schedule and cost milestones need to be established. These milestones must be appropriate to the type of project, e.g., exploratory research, product development. Notice the emphasis on demonstrable milestones. Many a project leader has been frustrated by a conscientious programmer who says, "I've practically completed the software module. I only have a few more lines of code left to do." After a few repetitions of this prognosis, the project leader may conclude that completion of coding is asymptotic at infinity. Project milestones must reflect a finite occurrence. Examples are satisfactory completion of a test, transfer of a tape from one organization to another, and issuance or signoff of a specification.

When estimating schedules and cost, a project leader may be getting into unfamiliar territory with AI technology. Various yardsticks have been prepared for level of effort required, the costs, and the time to develop the system (Anon., 1986). Several writers have estimated that obtaining a typical operational system may take three calendar years, require ten person-years of effort, and cost about a million dollars. Other experts have estimated that, depending on the size of the problem and the resources available, the time required to develop and field the system is one to three calendar years and from one to five person-years for development effort. Small systems would take less and big systems would require more. Some small systems have been developed for less than $100,000. Estimates of cost for system design and building are coming down with the availability of improved hardware and software as well as increased development efficiencies. One of the common measures of expert system complexity is the number of rules that it contains. If an approximate estimate of the final size of the system can be made, the time to develop it can be roughly estimated using a rule of thumb for a system production rate of one rule per hour per programmer. There is much disagreement about this figure and it is offered here only to indicate an order of magnitude. It is likely that this rule is correct for a 20-200 rule system written with the aid of a shell and that the time per rule will be much longer for very small and larger systems.

The need for a large amount of development effort for the non-AI component of the system is often overlooked. Much effort is required to integrate the AI portion into the balance of the system. This effort includes, among others, developing input-output (I/O) routines, data-base access, report generation, communications, security, and sensor interfaces. The user interface is a key element of the successful application of a knowledge system. The design and development of a satisfactory user interface can require from 25 to 50 percent of the total system software code.

The project plan must make provision for frequent changes in system design during development. This provision is not meant to condone a product specification which is a moving target, but rather to recognize that changes and reinterpretations in approach and content are almost inevitable. It is possible that substantial redesign will be required. Changes are particularly likely during the knowledge-elicitation and knowledge base building processes. During development of the system, the knowledge base and the control structure may become unwieldy, inefficient, or hard for the user to comprehend. It may then be advisable to incur the time and expense required to redesign or even reorient the scope of the problem. This has been referred to as "paradigm shift" (Hayes-Roth et al., 1983).

During the development cycle, the project leader may be faced with increasingly insistent demands that much of the initial prototype be scrapped. This is not necessarily an indication of ineptness on the part of the system developers. During the course of evaluating the initial prototype, it may be realized that the original problem definition was inaccurate or that the approach taken to solving the problem was not a good one.

There are, of course, trade-offs in incurring the cost and time for going from an 80 percent solution of the problem to a 98 percent solution. The primary value of the design effort for the initial prototype may turn out to be simply a training exercise. However, the initial prototype may also become the basis for totally different and valuable applications.

Another unanticipated cost for the project leader may be continuous growth in the size of the knowledge base. Elicitation and incorporation of an expanding body of knowledge into the system can be a continuing and expensive task. An example of such a knowledge domain might be a financial adviser system which must incorporate changes in financial products, economic environments, taxes, politics, etc. It is interesting to note that augmentation of the knowledge base does not necessarily deteriorate performance parameters such as throughput. It is possible that additional knowledge may decrease the system's search space, thereby increasing processing speed. It may also be true that at some stage in the design, a reorganization of the knowledge base may be necessary to increase processing speed.

STAFFING

Staffing an AI project is a significant challenge for a project leader. Most AI projects require a mix of skills different from those that are required for other development projects. Developing a fully qualified AI staff can be expensive and time consuming since both training and hands-on experience are required. Many courses and seminars are offered by universities and training organizations. The courses can vary in quality and checking references or talking to former attendees is suggested. If qualified instructors can be found, on-site training programs can offer advantages. Some of these advantages include:

1. More freedom to discuss and use company proprietary data and information during the course.

2. Reduced cost for travel and tuition if a relatively large number of people are to be trained.

3. Reduced demand on in-house manpower for training if the training period is expected to be short.

4. A curriculum (customized) for the purposes of the organization running the course.

Vendors of AI hardware and software also offer training. This training must be evaluated in the context of the vendor's goals. However, some of these programs provide excellent, if focused, training, particularly when they offer "hands-on" experience with hardware and software. Some government agencies offer financial support to companies which contract to train a specified number of employees in AI technology. Several larger organizations, particularly those which already have in-house training groups, have quite formal AI training programs.

In considering how much to invest in training, it should be remembered that there is a limit to the capability level that can be attained by attending training courses and seminars. As in most engineering disciplines, academic knowledge must be augmented by hands-on experience. After training, a skilled programmer, unfamiliar with AI languages and methods, will normally require six to nine months of intensive, hands-on experience to reach full proficiency. There is also, usually, a minimum number of people that should be actively working on the project. Experience at many organizations has placed this minimum number at three to five people, depending upon their skills. One highly skilled individual can have a strong positive catalytic effect on group performance and learning rate. A group can provide stimulating and effective interaction for its members, enabling them to reinforce each other in eliciting and interpreting information, and can support a comprehensive analysis of the various factors influencing hardware and software trade-offs. Some part-time project participants can also be helpful if a local labor pool is available. It is relatively easy to find skilled programmers in areas where educational institutions offer advanced training in AI. Of course, the labor pool may be considerably smaller elsewhere.

The project manager should also recognize that well-trained AI practitioners are still scarce, although there are many people with strong interest and good potential to become excellent workers. The danger of turnover as skills develop should not be ignored in evaluating compensation and morale factors within an AI group as it is trained.

As discussed in Chapter 4, an electronic communication system can be a useful tool. A universally available system facilitates interaction and can be more efficient than time-consuming meetings.

Changed attitudes and modes of operation among group members may also be required. During the history of AI research and application, there has been no shortage of towering egos, but developers of AI systems may have to learn much about humility. They must be amenable to change and endeavor to understand the thought processes and motivation of not only the user but also the source of the knowledge.

A project leader had worked hard to gain the understanding and cooperation of a well recognized domain expert. He had convinced the domain expert that this system would not be a threat to him, but would really make it easier for him to do his job. After some reluctance, the domain expert became an active participant. He provided much knowledge in a form that could be understood by the knowledge engineer and represented by the software specialists. After much hard work, an initial prototype was ready for demonstration to the domain expert. The project leader proudly brought the domain expert into the laboratory and sat him down in front of the CRT for an interactive session.

The system, using some canned data, asked the domain expert, "Is the pulse you are seeing wide?" The domain expert responded, "Yes, it is." A few questions later, the system asked the domain expert, "Is the pulse narrow?" The domain expert irritatedly responded, "No, it isn't, I told you it is wide." Unfortunately there were some further redundant questions of this type posed to the domain expert. Finally, in exasperation, the domain expert turned to the project leader and said, "This system isn't artificially intelligent, it's artificially stupid!"

The domain expert, of course, had a good point and served a large dose of humility to the developers of the system. Fortunately, the story had a happy ending; the developers were able to devise filters for redundant questions and arrange those asked by the system so that redundant questions would not be asked if a relevant answer had earlier been supplied to a similar question.

An available, competent and cooperative domain expert is a vital element in the success of a project. In addition to possessing the appropriate knowledge, the domain expert should be accepted as a qualified expert, particularly by the intended user. It is helpful, but not necessary, for the domain expert to have the communication skills to explain his or her knowledge to a knowledge engineer who may know little or nothing about the domain initially. Unfortunately, there may be many demands upon the time of the domain expert, thereby making that individual inaccessible to the AI project.

It is likely that even after the system has been fielded, there will be occasional further need for the expert. When an unanticipated condition occurs for which the knowledge base is incomplete, it might be necessary to call upon the expert for advice. The expert may not be familiar with the particular problem, but still be able to effectively reason out a solution.

If the AI project cannot be promised a sufficient allocation of the expert's time, it will be possible to start the project using a less experienced expert. The top expert can then be called in later to verify the knowledge that has been elicited. Another approach is to use an expert who is in or near retirement. Some of these individuals may be more readily available and even welcome the opportunity to "immortalize" their expertise.

In addition to having access to experts, it is necessary to keep them interested and enthusiastic during the development phase. They must be motivated to contribute even though some of the process appears repetitious or boring. They must be tolerant of the limitations of the system developers and the technology they use. The expert may not have an extensive theoretical background, and therefore suspicious of "schoolbook" or technologic approaches. Such experts must be continuously reassured of the value of their knowledge for the design of the system and the importance of their contribution to the organization.

There are many instances where the best source of detailed knowledge for an AI system is not at the upper levels of the technical or managerial organization chart. It is likely that the most useful knowledge will exist at or near the same level as that of the user. The senior manager may have a view of the overall objectives of the system that is not known at the operating level, but this is where the detailed procedural knowledge is most likely to be found. There may be a real difference in the way a particular job is perceived by senior management and the way that job is actually carried out. The wise knowledge engineer will recognize that more than one view of a task can exist, and in a sense, all views are correct. The real art in system design is to accommodate all views in the design so that the system does not, by its existence, force those involved to resolve their inconsistent approaches before they can accept the use of the system.

Vital and realistic background knowledge may be provided by long-time semiprofessional employees who truly understand the organization's procedures and its rules (some of which may actually be in conflict with each other). Gaining access to these employees may be complicated not only by the employee's attitude but also by managerial reluctance to provide such access. Nevertheless, these employees may be in the best position to explain how the job really is accomplished. These experts, as well as the more technically oriented professionals, may make frequent use of inexact knowledge. They will have difficulty in expressing just how they do their job. Their explanations could include such nonquantifiable terms as high and low, good and bad, hard and easy. They may also use conditionals such as, "If the boss really looks angry then I do this other job first." This is useful information although it may be difficult to represent in a computer system. Techniques such as fuzzy logic, described in Chapter 5, may be utilized.

Domain experts have reported an interesting result from their participation in the knowledge-elicitation process. Some have said that the elicitation process helped them improve their own understanding. It improved their way of looking at a problem and generating the solution. Some experts have also stated that as a result of participating in the process, they have improved their job performance and their ability to explain the procedures they are using.

Using multiple experts can be helpful in eliciting knowledge or in knowledge verification. But they can also introduce problems and complications (Mittal, 1985). Additional domain experts may help to clarify problems, improve the design of the user interface and increase user interest in the system. A second domain expert may be able to fill in gaps in the knowledge base or point out errors of interpretation.

Complications can arise when the experts do not agree with each other. On occasion, experts with differing opinions may each be right because each uses different approaches to solving a problem. Dealing with such differences poses a sensitive human relations issue for the project leader. As a result, many project leaders have concluded that it is better to attempt to utilize only one expert until the initial prototype has been completed. At this point, a second expert can be called in to verify systems operation and to fill in gaps in the knowledge. Experience shows that a skillful knowledge engineer can benefit from multiple sources of knowledge throughout much of the knowledge-elicitation and system-building process.

For many engineering organizations, the most difficult skill requirement to comprehend and to acquire may be that of the knowledge engineer. Why cannot the domain expert and knowledge engineer be the same person? This approach has been satisfactory in some situations, particularly if an appropriate software tool was available. More typically, however, different skills are required for these two positions. Also, it is difficult for the experts to effectively interview themselves. As discussed in Chapter 7, the rational, retrospective self-analysis of expertise is frequently incorrect.

A good knowledge engineer must have communication skills, patience, adaptability to new situations, an understanding of AI implementation techniques and an engaging personality. A good sense of humor is also helpful. It is unreasonable to expect a knowledge engineer to become a domain expert in a new field within a short time. However, the knowledge engineer must try to both value and understand the domain expert's basic concepts, buzz words, operating environment, and what information is important. This understanding will make the sessions with the domain expert run smoothly and efficiently.

In spite of developing a limited understanding of the domain, the knowledge engineer is still not the expert. For example, the knowledge engineer should not be the one responsible for selecting a particular alternative from among several proposed by different experts. Rather, he or she should attempt to find an approach that can accommodate all points of view. The knowledge engineer forms the bridge between the domain expert and the software specialist who will design the knowledge system.

Several AI projects in a large organization benefited from the contributions of an excellent knowledge engineer. This knowledge engineer had an educational background in the humanities rather than in computer science or engineering. This lack of theoretical technical knowledge was more than compensated for by outstanding communications skills. The knowledge engineer had a knack for interpreting how various experts performed their function and what knowledge was utilized in solving their problems. Another valuable capability was an adaptability to the different ways in which the experts expressed themselves. Some experts preferred written expositions; others used pictorial sketches and blackboard diagrams; still others paced the floor and related representative dialogues. Interestingly, this knowledge engineer was able to ask the experts "dumb" questions which would have irritated the expert if they had been posed by an individual with an engineering background.

Acquiring the human relations skills described above, while being highly desirable, is not necessarily a prerequisite for a successful AI development project. A dedicated staff, thoroughly familiar with their organization's activities and working in a supportive environment, may be able to develop a useful knowledge system.

A relatively small division of a large corporation had as a primary function the high-volume production of components with demanding specifications. The engineering staff did little computer development. Emphasis was on applying computers to a complex and sophisticated manufacturing process. Competitive pressures were intensifying and the plant manager determined that productivity would be improved by more "intelligent" monitoring of a vital process. Without the support of experienced AI specialists, the plant manager and a staff member did the knowledge elicitation and representation, coded the software in a high-order language, and implemented a knowledge system on a commercial computer. The resulting small expert system was instrumental in improving the productivity of a critical manufacturing process.

This success story is not representative of the majority of AI development projects. More frequently, skilled personnel and appropriate resources are required in order to meet project goals.

RAPID PROTOTYPING

Managers and technical personnel unfamiliar with AI are initially dubious about being able to develop even a limited-capability prototype in the space of just one or two months. (Rapid prototyping, in the jargon of the trade.) However, many rapid prototypes have been built in only a few weeks. These prototypes are necessarily limited in the degree to which they meet the overall requirements of the final system.

Rapid prototypes provide a number of significant benefits. The feasibility of the project plan can be verified before spending a major part of the budget. Meaningful discussions of functional requirements between the developers and users or customers can occur early in the project. These discussions can be helpful in reducing misunderstanding. Even with a detailed 500-page product specification, established and agreed upon at the beginning of a project, misunderstandings between developer and user can arise later in the project. It is difficult to perceive in advance all of the questions which may arise or differences in interpretation of what the specification means. When both developer and user are studying the same CRT screen output of a prototype, it is much easier to resolve differences on the scope of the problem, its solution, and the performance requirements for the system.

The initial prototype and its subsequent upgrades are helpful in assisting both the developer and the intended user to further define the subtleties of the problem. Many of these applications are in uncertain problem domains and the users themselves may be unsure of what the system should do and the environment in which it will operate. Since it is relatively easy to change the knowledge base in the prototype, further refinement of the user's thinking can be readily accommodated without causing substantial schedule and cost problems. If the extent of the requested modification becomes too great, the prototype can be used to evaluate the probability that the project constraints will be exceeded.

Even experienced AI project managers can be pleasantly surprised by the ease and speed with which a limited scope prototype can be developed.

A group of development engineers and manufacturing personnel had conceived of a knowledge system which they believed would be of great help to the quality assurance function. They explained the concept to a manager who only vaguely understood what the system would do. She agreed that the idea was certainly worth further study, but insisted that the concept be described more completely before development of even a demonstration-level prototype was started.

She stated to the development group, "Before we talk about funding you for this effort, please define the scope of the prototype. Give me a better feel for what this system will do and how much will be required to develop it." The development group was then charged with the responsibility, assisted by manufacturing, to write up a more detailed description of what they proposed to do. However, instead of writing up a definitive project specification, the development personnel went off by themselves. Two weeks later they called up the manager and asked her to come down to the laboratory. At that time, they were able to give her an effective demonstration that contained perhaps 15 or 20 rules. In the space of just two weeks, they were able to indicate both concept feasibility and potential benefits.

Although there are wide variations, a typical rule-based rapid prototype might comprise from 50 to 100 rules. Generally, building such a prototype requires one to three months of development time. The development time may be considerably shortened if effective software tools are utilized. Enthusiasm for immediate implementation of an operational system, generated by this short development time, must be tempered with reality regarding the capabilities of the prototype. Limitations of the first prototype may include:

1. Shallow knowledge inconsistent with a full-scale system

2. Ability to handle only one or two limited test cases

3. Inefficient implementation

4. Constrained user interface

5. System operation requiring supervision by the developer

As noted in Chapter 8, it is desirable to select an AI project which can subsequently also serve as a building block for additional applications. The rapid prototype can be an effective vehicle to provide a basis for considering other applications. Evaluation and use of the prototype frequently generates other ideas, either from the domain expert or from the intended user. Some of these new ideas may go considerably beyond the intended scope of the first AI project (Bachant and McDermott, 1984).

PROJECT PHASES

General statement

The project plan should reflect the fact that there are a number of phases entailed in the development of an AI system. These phases may be explicitly related, they may be overlapping, or there may be initially some uncertainty as to the need for inclusion of some of the project phases. The project plan should be appropriate for the type of system being developed. The plan for an R&D project should provide for considerable flexibility in execution of the various project phases. A commercial, industrial, or military project would require a more carefully structured plan that describes goals, schedules, demonstrable milestones, responsibilities, and funding allocations. These project phases need not be set in concrete, but should be continually updated so that they reflect the current approach for all interested parties. For some applications, it may be inevitable that there is frequent restructuring of the system design, including its functions, during the development. Since it may be difficult to predict these iterations in advance, it can be helpful to establish milestones indicating the points at which change or continuation decisions will be made. The fact that these iterations can be unpredictable makes it even more imperative to maintain some sort of configuration control on the system. Several authors have provided detailed descriptions of the implementation steps in developing AI systems (Harmon, 1986; Smith, 1984).

Table 11.1 presents a sequence of project phases. Depending on the type of project and the application, some of these phases may be eliminated or their sequence changed. Also, there may not be a clear demarcation between the individual project phases. For example, the knowledge-acquisition phase will not be completed before beginning the implementation. In fact, during the design of the system the knowledge base will almost certainly have to be changed. Also, several iterations of knowledge gathering, building of prototypes and testing will be required.

Analysis

Please refer to Table 11.1. After project go-ahead has been received, the problem must be defined in greater detail. It is recognized, of course, that there may be circumstances where application definition cannot be completed until additional knowledge is acquired and user interactions are defined more completely. At any rate, require-

---

TABLE 11.1   AI Development Project Phases

Analysis
1. Initial application definition
2. Project plan
3. Commitment of resources
4. First-cut selection of hardware and software (for development and delivery)
5. Limited-scope knowledge acquisition
6. Knowledge representation
7. Preliminary system design and coding
8. Demonstration or proof-of-concept prototype

Design
1. Refinement of application definition
2. Project plan upgrade
3. Confirmation or modification of hardware and software selection and acquisition
4. Knowledge acquisition
5. Detailed design
6. Prototype building
7. Evaluation using limited scope examples
8. User, marketing, and other functional inputs
9. Detailed application definition

Decisions
1. Use, modify, or scrap the prototype
2. Project plan upgrade

Verification and Delivery
1. Knowledge acquisition
2. Complete detailed design
3. Test and validation
4. User training
5. Field test
6. Release and delivery
7. Maintenance

---

ments should be defined sufficiently to enable preparation of a project plan. This project plan should not be written solely for archival purposes. Rather, it should be dynamic, providing direction and understanding for all participants during the project. In addition to the project plan, there are traditional software development project document formats which may be tailored to be appropriate. These include standards for design, coding, integration, quality assurance, and documentation. Elements of this project plan dealing with knowledge elicitation have been described in Chapter 7. In addition to the specifics of application requirements, the project plan must also describe the needed resources and when they must be available.

Establishing the resource requirements probably requires the initial selection of hardware and software to be used for development and for the delivery vehicle. It may be premature to make a final selection at the start of the project, but it is difficult to do further product planning and design without at least some attention to the capabilities and limitations of hardware and software that will be used.

The next phase of the project, knowledge acquisition, may be one of the most difficult, particularly when the project team is first becoming familiar with AI technology. Domain experts and knowledge engineers with the appropriate skills must be made available. A plan of action must be formulated for eliciting the knowledge. When the knowledge base is sufficient to at least broadly define the problem and its proposed solutions, the knowledge-representation phase should begin. This phase may proceed concurrently with additional knowledge acquisition, particularly, if the personnel working on knowledge representation are not the same as those working on knowledge acquisition. It is during the knowledge-representation phase that the architecture of this system is developed. In addition to the requirements of the problem and its solutions, the knowledge-representation methodology employed should reflect the parameters of software tools being used, the higher-order language selected, user interfaces, requirements, time and cost constraints, market pressures and the experiences and preferences of the developers. When the methodology for representing the knowledge is determined, system design and coding may begin. System design and coding should be strongly influenced by the software and hardware being utilized as well as the experience of the development personnel. System design and software coding may be structured to produce a proof-of-concept or demonstration prototype early in the project. Once reactions to the prototype are available, design and coding can continue.

Design

User, domain expert and "check-signer" reactions to the prototype should provide a basis for refining the project plan and problem definition. There may also be important input from other functional areas such as management and marketing. With a more complete understanding of the project requirements and a suitable approach, the selection of the hardware and software to be used for both the development phase and for the delivery system can be confirmed. Evaluation of the demonstration prototype also indicates where additional knowledge is needed. Contradictions and gaps in knowledge can be resolved. Detailed design is then undertaken. The output of this detailed design effort is a usable prototype. This prototype typically would not be intended for delivery to a user, but should be complete enough to provide a thorough demonstration of the ultimate system performance and user interface. Sample limited-scope problems are run on this prototype. Both the domain expert and the user should confirm that the prototype satisfactorily solves such limited-scope problems.

Decisions

Based upon demonstrations and experience with the prototype, additional requirements and comments may be received from the user, marketing, or other functional areas. The application of the AI system may now be defined in considerable detail. A decision point is then reached. Should the prototype design be the basis for the deliverable system, or should the design be modified or even scrapped? Having made this decision, any required changes to the knowledge base and the detailed design are completed.

Verification and delivery

Upon completing the detailed design, the system must be tested and validated. (Procedures for testing and validating the system are described in Chapter 12.) Prior to releasing the system for delivery, it may be a good idea to begin user training on the system. This will ease the transition between the developer and user, generate additional valuable input on system features and make the user an active champion for success of the project. When the system has been sufficiently tested and validated, it is time for field testing. Depending upon the complexity and application of the system, field testing may approach the sophistication of the Alpha and Beta test levels of large computer hardware and software systems. A less rigorous field test may be adequate for smaller or specialized systems. Upon completion of the field testing, the system is then released for delivery. This release should be accompanied by a careful plan for maintaining the system.

To summarize, including some or all of the project phases, as described above, may be appropriate. The scope of the problem, the experience of developers, and input from users and other functional organizations influence the choice of these project phases. There probably will be no clear demarcation between completion of one phase and beginning of another. It may also be appropriate to repeat some of the phases. Flexibility in managing the project is essential. However, the project should not be operated so loosely that participants are unsure of what is required of them. Also, management must be confident that the project is being operated in consonance with the constraints placed on it.

KEEPING IT SOLD

During the early phases of the AI development project, the project leader is sometimes faced with the dismaying need to resell the project. Even though initial go-ahead was received and the project is proceeding well, it may become necessary to justify the continuing use of equipment or personnel resources. More distressing is the prospect of a cutoff in funding. Even after a successful demonstration of the initial prototype, reconsideration of funding may be caused by still lingering skepticism about the potential for the technology or the pressure from other, seemingly more urgent short-term priorities.

Another reality, common to many organizations, is the frequent regroupings which can change relationships and responsibilities while the knowledge system is being developed. In any event, continuous selling may be required throughout the project. It must continue to demonstrate finite achievements to management during development.

The project plan should include milestones for highlighting these achievements, even if they are not "earth-shaking." A dynamic project plan can also be the basis for continuing negotiation between the project manager and other levels of management. Management, of course, must continue to be sold, but also users and other functional organization must remain supportive. The technical merits of an AI application are not always sufficient to keep the project funded.

An AI group developed a simulator which potentially had a number of advantages over the algorithmic simulator being run on the mainframe computer. Unfortunately, the project phases entailed in going from initial prototype to a deliverable system were never completed. There were several problems which precluded completion of the project. One of the intended user groups had not actively participated in the early development phases. Their reaction was, "That's really not the way we design things. This new simulator of yours won't really do us any good." The project also suffered from misunderstandings on what was to be accomplished in the early phases of the project. As is typical in many AI applications, there were numerous uncertainties when the project was started.

The project goals and project milestones should have been continually refined. These refinements should have been discussed with all of the participants and interested parties, particularly those who were ultimately responsible for funding the balance of the project. The project was also adversely affected because there were too many starts and redirections. A realistic plan should have been developed, published, and widely disseminated earlier in the project. It would then have been possible to modify this project plan as needed and in concert with the rest of the organization.

Although it can be distracting and time consuming, the project manager must be sensitive to any need for reselling the project. A useful vehicle for reselling is a good demonstration of the initial prototype. If this prototype has adequate graphics, it can be effective in convincing skeptics. It can be limited in its capabilities, but it should have a user interface which is effective as a selling tool. Permitting skeptics to experiment with the prototype is also useful. The demonstration should enable skeptics to grasp what is unique about AI technology. Good impressions are also generated by being able to readily modify elements of the knowledge base and their relationships. The demonstration need not be specific to the activities of the viewers, but they should be able to relate it to their own interests. A good demonstration may, furthermore, trigger ideas for still other applications.

A supporting technique is the recounting of success stories in AI technology, particularly those from competitors or important customers. Another effective selling tool is a professionally produced videotape. For some applications, a videotape can have a greater impact than observing the CRT screen on a demonstration system. The tape can illustrate how the job is currently done and contrast it with the benefits of using the knowledge system. It can also speed up the presentation so that important points are made rapidly to busy people. The tape can also be given to people to view at their convenience. Finally, an enthusiastic domain expert is a valuable assistant in the selling process.

Implementing the Project

USER INVOLVEMENT

Previous chapters have referred to the importance of having the eventual user of a knowledge system actively involved in development of the project. At times this involvement may be inconvenient or impractical since the intended user may be unknown or unavailable or, at the moment, oblivious of what will be developed for him or her. Note also that the eventual "owner" of the system is not necessarily the user. (An example is a knowledge system for which the MIS department has responsibility.) It is particularly helpful if the intended user can provide some of the development funding. This increases the commitment to making the project successful. Where it is feasible, involving the user early in the project increases the probability that the project will be successful when fielded.

User involvement is desirable in most projects, not just for AI projects. The benefits of this philosophy have been well established, for example, in software development, as a means of uncovering misunderstandings and preventing problems during early phases of the project rather than a year or so later when the system is finally delivered. Using this philosophy is even more important in AI projects where there are many unknowns and uncertainties.

It is not enough merely to invite users in for a conference at the beginning of the project. Users, even after the intent of the system is explained to them, still may not be sure just what their roles should be. Why should they be at all interested in having the project succeed? The system developer must determine user needs and meet them with the system design as well as help develop user interest in the project. A positive reaction may be obtained from users if the potential of a knowledge system to assist them in increasing their level of responsibility is described. However, the user may still be concerned about being put in the spotlight in a new project with unknown risk. Remember that many intended users may never have been actively involved in a research and development project, and it could be an unsettling experience for them.

The development team should be able to clearly explain the application and benefits of the system to the intended user, particularly if the user is not the domain expert. If a clear explanation cannot be provided, then perhaps the project's goals should be re-evaluated.

PRODUCT FEATURES

User interface

Once the active cooperation of the intended user is gained, it is then incumbent upon the system designers to devote adequate resources to be certain that the system has an effective user interface. An effective interface is particularly important if the user is not likely to be an expert in the field. System design is particularly challenging if there is a wide technical or cultural gap between the domain expert and the nontechnical user. For example, prior to the building of the system, the domain expert may have provided recommendations or directions to others or may have fixed the problem without help. If it is replacing the expert in some situations, the knowledge system must replace the approach used by the domain expert and provide needed support to the nontechnical user. As it is used, the knowledge system must appear compatible with the thought processes, procedures, and environment of the actual end user of the system.

The effort entailed in developing such an interface can easily exceed that required to elicit and represent the knowledge. Nevertheless, this is still an essential design requirement since the part of the system that the user most comes into contact with is usually the I/O. The subtleties of a sophisticated reasoning methodology will not pacify a user who is irritated because of the awkward presentation of a menu on a CRT screen.

Compatibility with user requirements

What the user really wants or needs when using the system may not always be obvious or in agreement with the objectives of the management.

A knowledge engineer was told by the expert that her job was to find which one of several common problems had occurred by asking questions over the phone. The user, on the other hand, said that he was able to recognize these common problems himself and normally consulted the expert only when the problem that was found was unusual and did not fit any of these common problem types.

Some questions that are important to answer include:

1. Do the user's stated desires conflict with what would be a better problem solution?

2. Will the user's approach potentially be harmful rather than helpful?

3. Should the interaction with the system be designed for a naive or experienced user, or both?

As has been previously emphasized, the primary requirement for the knowledge system to support may be to assist individuals in doing a better job, or to improve their work environment. This more limited goal can have a substantial influence on the size of the project since it is no longer necessary to automate all the human functions performed by either the user or the expert.

Users may also be initially unfamiliar with another aspect of current knowledge systems. These systems do not necessarily provide the best answer to a problem, but rather may only provide a solution which can be considered satisfactory or adequate. While a less-than-best solution may be perfectly acceptable in many applications, it is important that in subsequent use of the system using the same input data, the same answer is provided to the users. Otherwise, if the users receive different answers to what they perceive to be the identical problem, confusion and frustration will arise.

Explanation facility

An effective explanation capability is of great value to the user, particularly for use by non-experts or for remotely fielded systems. The explanation capability should be available to the user in a readily understood format which is consistent and accurate. The help feature should be tiered, that is, available to the user in increasing levels of detail. In this way, the help feature can be responsive to both novice and experienced user.

As described in Chapter 4, some explanation systems have been ineffective because they merely provided a listing of the rule firing order and a text of difficult-to-comprehend rules that were used in the program to reach a conclusion. Such a system is much more useful to the developer than the ultimate user. Other systems have erred in a different direction, that is, overwhelming the user with more than is really wanted. For example, the user may not be particularly interested in the full details of the reasoning used but only to check that the answer provided can be used or relied upon. For some users, there may be truth in the premise that: "People don't want to reason—they just want to know the answer!"

Progress is being made in providing systems that are easier to understand (Neches et al., 1985). Sometimes there may be some value in showing the user the logic or "thought process" that the system used in arriving at its conclusions if this can be done in an understandable manner. This feature can increase the user's confidence in the answers provided by the system. The feature may make it easier for the user to modify the system recommendations to fit the particular set of circumstances at hand.

An example of good explanation facilities can be found in some commercially available financial systems (Kosy, 1986). The improving capabilities of natural language systems should further improve the quality of explanation systems (McKlowin *et al.*, 1985; Vilnat and Sabah, 1985). There are some early research efforts showing progress in developing systems which reason in a manner similar to that used by humans (Bouwman, 1983).

System interfaces

Knowledge systems usually must have an appropriate interface to both existing non-AI systems and the user. Knowledge systems frequently are not intended to be a stand-alone product. For example, an expert system might have a natural language front end to accept input from the user and be connected to a data base to receive information. An added feature for a natural language front end might be a voice recognition capability which would be particularly attractive for "hands-busy" inspection. The system designer must use an approach consistent with the specific details of how external sources like data bases are accessed or processes are controlled. Incorporating a knowledge system into a larger system requires consideration of all significant integration parameters. For example, a diagnostic system might require close coupling with related maintenance and spare parts procedures. The system may also have to be hardware and software compatible with existing automatic test equipment (Powell *et al.*, 1986). Providing such capability may take a substantial amount of development effort and software coding.

Implementation languages

The issue of which higher-order software language should be used in implementing knowledge systems has been debated continuously with almost religious fervor. There are many pros and cons but, as yet, no consensus has developed for a particular language or dialect. It is beyond the scope of this chapter to detail the advantages and disadvantages of the various languages being used. In general, however, LISP and PROLOG have been the most frequently used languages for development of knowledge systems, particularly large ones. There have been numerous examples of converting software codes initially written in LISP to more widely used languages. The intent of such conversions is usually to obtain greater portability and ease of maintenance. It may be easier to maintain a complex system in LISP. Sometimes the pressure to use another language comes from customers or is due to the lack of programmers sufficiently skilled in LISP or PROLOG. Systems written in these two languages have been converted into C, ADA, FORTRAN, PL1, and APL.

OBTAINING A GOOD PRODUCT

System design objectives

Development of a knowledge system should not be assumed to be only a software coding activity. It is important that the project have frequent participation of a systems-oriented engineer who can understand and present the "big picture." The engineer must have, in addition to knowledge of the technical issues, a sensitivity to the opinions of designers, domain experts, users, and other functional organizations such as finance and marketing. Such other views may be well intentioned and spurred by the anticipation that AI might also be able to do something for their organization.

A frequent problem in such circumstances is to bound the objectives of the initial prototype. Consideration of other applications should certainly be encouraged, but demonstrations of broader capability should not be allowed to interfere with meeting the project's objectives within the existing constraints. Given these pressures and in order to minimize misunderstanding, the project manager should obtain agreement and commitments from users, "owners" of resources, and domain experts. These agreements and commitments include system performance as well as resource requirements.

Satisfying the requirements for extensive I/O features, as well as additional extrapolations of the originally intended application, may cause the knowledge system to become too complex. This can be a particular problem in building prototypes. If the system does become unwieldy, it may be feasible to divide it into subsystems. Then, separate and more tractable knowledge systems can be developed for each module. This is also a good technique when application requirements or the knowledge base are likely to change during development.

For some applications which are large scale and have a potentially high payoff, it is impractical to prepare a definitive product specification when initiating the project. It may be difficult to describe the various activities which will be eventually impacted by the knowledge system. For example, in a manufacturing planning system, the products and the production processes may be quite variable and change frequently. One solution for this problem is to make knowledge system performance more responsive by utilizing a high level of abstraction in the system design. This permits users to particularize their interactions to fit specific problems (Kline and Dolins, 1986).

Knowledge management

Various techniques have been used for representing and manipulating the knowledge in an AI system. There are many technical and performance trade-offs involved in selecting a technique. A large body of technical literature is available which describes methods for implementation and utilization of AI technology. Recently a set of guidelines has been developed under a government contract intended to assist an expert system designer in selecting an appropriate AI implementation technique (Semeco *et al.*, 1986). These guidelines discuss the type of reasoning to be used, search methodology, and also provide estimates of the magnitude of the project.

KEEPING THE PROJECT ON TRACK

A plan of the type described in Chapter 11 should guide the management of the project. The project leader, of course, must make continued trade-offs between rigid adherence to the project plan and responding to changing requirements or constraints. The degree of flexibility required is influenced by the type of development project, the occurrence of unanticipated circumstances, and various constraints placed upon the project. A satisfactory compromise between conflicting objectives may be aided by problem decomposition.

There is frequent pressure to take shortcuts in the development cycle. Reasons presented for taking shortcuts include:

1. Schedule or budget problems

2. Lack of information

3. Complexity of the application or the system's implementation

4. Conflicting objectives

5. Other priorities or interests

Realistically, some of these shortcuts may be taken even if they do increase the risk of not meeting all project constraints. The problem of assessing the risk of using shortcuts is compounded by the degree of uncertainty which is still characteristic of the AI development process. There is also a risk of being sidetracked by the explosive rate of technologic advance and product improvement.

In order to maintain schedules without overly stifling creativity, ideas for product improvements can be stored in an electronic filing system for later consideration. An electronic filing system is also useful for documenting solutions to development problems and the rationale for decisions that were made.

VALIDATION

Testing

The primary purpose of the validation phase of the project is to determine if the system does what it is supposed to do. This is not always obvious. In order to insure satisfactory performance of the knowledge system, realistic test cases must be developed. If the system developers or end users are not domain experts, letting them employ the system to solve several sample problems can provide a preliminary validation. This is particularly helpful in pointing out gaps in the knowledge base or reasoning process. Many of the validation procedures used with conventional software projects are also applicable to AI software. These include walk-throughs, functional testing, and various types of reviews. Conducting numerous "little tests" may uncover errors and problems which would be missed in an overall systems test.

Validation of an AI system is an important issue throughout the system life cycle to a much greater extent than with conventional software. Since the behavior of large and complex knowledge-based systems cannot be predicted totally in advance when the knowledge base is modified, careful validation is required after each modification.

In some situations the testing can be done effectively only after the system has been delivered to the field. In other situations, a satisfactory level of confidence can be obtained prior to shipment. In either case, it is essential that the system be subjected to the problems and environment for which it was designed.

The procedures and methodology for validating the system are also a function of the application. A research and development project will require a less stringent process than a medical or military system. Depending on the application, various approaches will be appropriate. It may be satisfactory to insert simple test cases and verify the expected results. More complex applications may require test scenarios with a panel of experts evaluating the results. This may include statistical analysis of the percentage of solutions which are correct, acceptable, or unacceptable. Analytic software tools may be used to check for redundant or conflicting rules, explanation tracing, and accesses made to the knowledge base or the inference mechanism. Detailed testing evaluates rule firings, characterizations of objects, graphics, and interfaces to other software and hardware.

There are other reasons for insisting that an adequate testing phase be included in the project plan. For example, a thorough testing program may uncover conflicting rules that have been incorporated in the knowledge base. These conflicts may not be caused by a mistake on the part of the system developer. Actually, the conflicts may accurately reflect input from the domain expert (perhaps at different times during the knowledge-elicitation process). How does the expert respond when confronted with these conflicts in practice? Perhaps the expert uses some modifying information which was not explicitly stated during knowledge elicitation.

An expert system was developed to aid in the identification of concealed objects in a photograph. When provided with the relevant input data, the expert system identified the object as a Model 42 truck. The expert when presented with this result objected, saying it was incorrect. The system designer protested that it was in accordance with the rules they had been given. The expert then responded that account had not been taken of the fact that the truck had a sloping hood. This made it a Model 95. It was then necessary to augment the knowledge base with this new information which had been uncovered during the testing phase.

Even with a good predelivery test phase, problems may arise soon after initial delivery. During the early phases of field use, additional mistakes or gaps will be found in the knowledge system. However, it is probably not a good idea to delay field introduction until every conceivable element of the knowledge is complete. Some inadequacies in a complex system just will not be uncovered until the system is put into actual use.

Validation criteria

Establishing specific criteria for successful system performance is also a judgmental issue. It may be necessary to accept systems that occasionally make some less-than-optimum recommendations, or even occasional mistakes. It should be remembered that human experts also make mistakes sometimes. It is better to provide mechanisms that can assist the user in detecting, correcting or ignoring incorrect answers. Note also that in some applications, a system can still be useful if it meets only some of the acceptance criteria. Such a system might be delivered for limited use while being redesigned to meet the remaining requirements.

More specific criteria can be established with regard to the user interface. Again, these criteria may be somewhat subjective but arbitrary decisions on acceptability must be made. Is the user interface appropriate to the environment in which it will be used? Do users become irritated by the manner in which questions are posed to them on the CRT screen? More difficult is the evaluation of the reasoning process the system used in arriving at a conclusion or solving a problem. However, such an evaluation can assist the user in determining the reliability of the response given by the system. It may not be practical to place a numeric rating on the performance of the knowledge system's reasoning process. After all, ratings are usually not applied to a human expert's performance as an attorney, physician, or electronics technician (Hayes-Roth *et al.*, 1983).

Error reporting

In verifying the performance of a field system, problems may be encountered in collecting performance data, particularly the specifics on errors. Enforcing a complete error-reporting discipline can be frustrating since the system users frequently have other demands on their time. Where feasible, some sort of automated error-reporting process should be incorporated in the system design. Automated error reporting has the added value of providing a basis for statistics on the circumstances of error occurrences. Such statistics can be important input for making changes in the knowledge base or design of the system.

FIELD SUPPORT

Level of support

As is the case with many other computer-based products, knowledge systems may require extensive support after the product has been delivered to the user. In fact, these systems may require, at least initially, a disproportionately high level of support. Part of this is due to the newness of the technology or that the system output may be more subjective than other computer systems. Retaining the confidence of the user is important and this confidence would be eroded if system maintenance were inadequate. Maintaining user confidence is even more important if the primary purpose of the system is to improve the performance of the user. In order to improve maintenance, some developers of knowledge systems have delegated this responsibility to the data processing or MIS group. These groups may be more experienced and better organized to provide ongoing maintenance. Annual maintenance costs can exceed the system development cost, but more typically they are in the range from 10 to 25 percent. This annual proportion is higher for small systems.

Training

The project plan must take into account the extent of training needed by the user. How will this training be provided? The vendors of some software packages, for example, provide several training courses of increasing complexity and technical sophistication.

Training is costly and time consuming but necessary if the user is to obtain full system benefits. For example, a user may understand an expert system's individual rules, but not their linkage into an overall reasoning process. Gaining complete understanding of system operation is particularly important where "ownership" of the system is to be eventually transferred to the user. Such users must be adequately trained in order to accept responsibility for operating and maintaining their system.

Various approaches to training have been utilized. For systems incorporating AI technology, "hands-on" training is particularly effective. AI systems can be provided with good graphics capabilities and an interactive mode of training. Some graphics presentations are dynamic, complete with gauges and meters which react in response to questions or problems posed to the trainee (Hollan *et al.*, 1984).

Many knowledge systems are designed to operate with extensive interaction with the user. In order to obtain satisfactory performance from the system, the user must be fairly familiar with the means to access the various capabilities of the system. There have been examples of users being given training in the operation of the system, but in essence, missing the entire first week of the training because they did not really understand just how to turn the system on and off! Even after participating in a good vendor training program, it can be difficult to understand and use all the features of a complex machine or software package. A more complete understanding is acquired by experience or osmosis, that is, using the feature under the guidance of someone else.

A cost which may be overlooked in planning the project is that entailed in preparing training materials. If computer-aided instruction (CAI) is to be used, developing the courseware can be expensive. For each hour of student interaction, the development cost can exceed $10,000. Expert systems and software tools are being developed to reduce this cost (Freedman and Rosenking, 1986). Another deterrent to more widespread application of these intelligent tutoring systems is their lack of generalization. Some of these systems have been difficult to adapt to other domains.

Maintenance

An important feature of knowledge systems is the capability for upgrading them after the initial design has been completed. The application may require the incorporation of additional "real-world knowledge" during the entire life of the system. This process, however, must be controlled in order to avoid serious problems. Procedures must be established and enforced for the incorporation of new knowledge. These procedures should specify maintenance responsibilities and, as an example, who is permitted to make changes in the knowledge base. Particular caution must be exercised on field updates which can create conflicts with existing rules or precipitate dead-end searches through the knowledge base. If numerous field modifications to the knowledge base are anticipated, it may be desirable to incorporate a knowledge base checking system (Nguyen *et al.*, 1985). The system may contain built-in design constraints on the type and magnitude of field modifications that can be made. Also included may be a trigger mechanism for ensuring concurrence by the project manager in any changes recommended by field users. These constraints on field modification may be particularly necessary when the user does not have a detailed understanding of how the system represents and manipulates the knowledge. For example, seemingly minor differences in syntax can cause subtle and difficult-to-find problems.

Hardware and Software

STATUS AND PROJECTIONS

Computer designers and manufacturers are creating an almost insatiable demand for greater memory and higher processing speeds, by expanding capability while simultaneously reducing the cost of the hardware. Semiconductor and computer manufacturers have programs to develop new or improved microprocessors and architectures optimized for AI applications. With the technology advancing so rapidly, proposed applications that are now limited by what is available in delivery hardware and software may become more cost-effective by the time the system is fielded one or two years later. Cost-to-performance ratios of systems which include an embedded AI segment will be enhanced by VLSI "LISP on a chip" implementations.

Certainly, the implementation of some complex AI applications are being paced by the lack of specialized architectures, parallel processing and different types of software. But for many other applications, the required improvement in hardware can realistically be assumed to be available by the time the system is to be delivered to the user (Highberger and Edson, 1984). Important advances are also being made in software methodology. These advances in software and hardware technology result from:

- Recognition of a potentially large and profitable market
- Academic research
- Government requirements
- Industrial research
- Response to shortened product life cycles
- Programs of national consortia (MCC, Alvin, Esprit, ICOT)
- Recognition of significance of information technology

While accurate predictions of the schedules for advances in hardware and software are difficult to make, some trends are discernible. For example, the extensive government and academic research on different types of computing architectures will eventually produce the type of processing power and capability required by complex AI systems. Machines featuring increasingly massive parallelism are being introduced, although they are currently cost-effective only for specialized applications, primarily because of the difficulty of writing efficient software for them. Finding methods to use the large body of software that has been written for nonparallel machines under parallel conditions appears to be even more difficult although research on optimizing compilers is underway.

However, some of these development programs are affecting hardware and software development in the near-term. Widespread introduction of these specialized architecture machines is deterred by the substantial installed base of conventional systems. These installed systems represent a large investment in hardware and even more in software. Users must have good reason to discard this large investment. Since an ever increasing number of symbolic processors are being acquired, it seems likely that users are finding ways to make use of both conventional and specialized architectures.

Continuing advances may be anticipated in more conventional computer technology such as:

- Rapid fall in costs of memory and computation power
- More effective use of shared resources and capabilities (expensive printers, mass storage, etc.)
- More user-friendly
- Improved programming environments
- Cost-effective workstations
- Automation of routine development tasks
- Wider acceptance of software and hardware standards

A word of caution is in order. Many of these advances anticipate extraordinary achievements in semiconductor technology. However, it must be remembered that the availability of a high-powered CPU chip is only one ingredient in an advanced AI system architecture. Similarly, the CPU chip is only one element of the total cost of a workstation.

DEVELOPMENT HARDWARE

General statement

An AI development system is primarily intended for use in discovering and characterizing knowledge, rather than for delivering it. In some applications, it may be feasible to also use the development hardware and software in the fielded system. As noted below, this feasibility is influenced by various factors such as cost and physical environment. An analogy to development and delivery systems is the distinction between start-up and production tooling.

Dedicated systems

There has been a preference for utilizing dedicated hardware and software for developing AI systems. The hardware is variously referred to as LISP machines, symbolic processors, or dedicated machines. The general attitude has been that greater performance as well as increased efficiency in the development process can be achieved by using hardware specifically designed for the purpose. This attitude has been reinforced by the continuing drop in prices of specialized machines. It had been necessary to invest from $75,000 to $150,000 in symbolic processors and software tools in order to do serious AI development work. For many organizations, this was difficult to justify, particularly since such systems could typically be used by only one person at a time. However, use of dedicated machines is becoming more cost-effective, because the prices have been dropping rapidly. In addition to the benefits of processing power, graphics, and other architectural features, these dedicated systems frequently feature an extensive and powerful programming environment. They include software utilities and analysis tools which greatly expedite the development of complex knowledge systems. As compared to what is available on personal computers, the larger specialized machines can accommodate much larger knowledge bases and more sophisticated manipulation of knowledge.

Mainframes

Until recently, a mainframe computer, unless used in a dedicated mode, was not considered suitable for developing AI software. A general-purpose, time-sharing system would be overloaded by the large overhead requirements of an AI language development environment and operating system so the economics favored a special-purpose machine.

One company was formed to develop and produce an AI-based system for training applications. The target market for this product were owners of large mainframe computers. Development of the product was carried out on a high-end LISP machine and successfully completed. Unfortunately, the developers were unable to obtain adequate processing speed in the mainframe and the company was forced to restructure under rather difficult conditions for both the investors and employees of the company.

It is certainly possible to develop and deliver many AI systems on conventional computer mainframes or minicomputers. In fact, many of the original and successful applications of AI were developed on conventional computers using conventional software. Considerable controversy has been generated on the subject of using conventional machines. Proponents insist that conventional machines with good LISP compilers can run AI programs as well as specialized symbolic processors. This is disputed by many AI developers who question the quality of the software and development environment provided by conventional machine vendors. They also claim that there is too much reliance on third-party developers (Davis, 1986). The attitude of many AI systems developers is that symbolic processors are superior to conventional processors in development features and operating capability.

The advantage of conventional machines, of course, is their widespread availability, familiarity and cost per user. They also have a better track record than the LISP machines for reliability, maintenance and other customer service features. Primarily for these reasons, LISP machines have had difficulty in penetrating the office environment. In addition to surmounting the *status quo* hurdles, users of LISP machines have had technical problems relating to connectivity and these machines have not been able to do some simple office functions.

Conventional mainframes will have an important role as delivery vehicles. Much of the data needed by knowledge systems is available only on mainframes so that cost and connectivity issues will drive the selection of these delivery methods.

Other users may insist on development on mainframes for security reasons. Many installations have elaborate security procedures already in use. Knowledge systems may, indeed, utilize sensitive information and it could be expensive to duplicate the same security procedures that have already been developed for the mainframe computers.

Hybrid systems

As noted in Chapter 5, most AI systems are now being developed for use in specific applications rather than for demonstrations or proof of principle. Also, the AI portion of the system may be embedded in a larger system built with conventional software methods. This requirement will normally force the developer of the system to use conventional types of hardware and software. However, there are some types of applications where the requirements of the application will force the user to use some form of hybrid system where the symbolic processing is done on a specialized machine and the more conventional data-base and I/O operations on conventional-architecture machines. The problems of interfacing associated with the use of such a mixed system are being considered by some manufacturers of AI systems but much work remains to be done. Some of the particular applications where the capability of specialized machines will likely be required include:

1. Large knowledge bases

2. Stand-alone, single-purpose systems

3. Systems with realtime, complex reasoning features

Workstations

There is a pronounced trend, particularly for vendors of AI software tools, to port their LISP-oriented systems to widely available workstations. Although these workstations may not have all of the features of the larger symbolic processors, the necessary compromises are not too severe for many applications. Top-of-the-line engineering workstations are challenging market segments dominated by symbolic processors (Verity, 1986). These workstations have good graphics capability and considerable computer processing power. Importantly, they are oriented towards user requirements. They have a large I/O bandwidth and include such features as memory management and data manipulation. Most workstation manufacturers are working with third-party suppliers of AI systems and languages to provide a capability equivalent to that of symbolic processors on their machines. Providing a development environment equivalent to that of symbolic processors has been the most difficult problem for these third-party suppliers.

Personal computers

With the continuing proliferation and increasing cost effectiveness of personal computers (PC), there is much interest in developing knowledge systems on these machines. Many useful applications can be developed on small machines (Hewett and Sasson, 1986). Implementation on a PC can also be helpful in defining the scope and establishing the feasibility of a project which will eventually be designed and built on a larger system.

Another application of a PC-based knowledge system is its use as a learning tool. These learning tools can be quite effective but, typically, they are capable of representing only a segment of what can be achieved with AI technology.

Migration

If the project plan does call for the more usual migration of the development system from a symbolic processor to a PC, a number of design factors should be considered. Subsets of development languages are available on the PC, which greatly assist in porting the system from the large machine to the PC. However, troublesome bugs in the software are possible when this porting takes place. Also, some of the features which would be useful on the large system are not available on the PC, perhaps resulting in a less-than-optimum product.Well-qualified knowledge engineers and software specialists are needed to insure an effective transition from the symbolic processor to the small machine.

A particular problem is the user interface. It is difficult to obtain the same extensive graphics capability on most PCs as are readily available on symbolic processors.

SOFTWARE TOOLS

It has been suggested that the widespread application of knowledge systems is contingent on continuing advances in hardware. From the standpoint of the developer of knowledge systems, the key breakthrough has been the introduction of software development tools and shells. Perhaps three-quarters of the nonacademic expert systems discussed in the literature were developed with the aid of expert-system building tools. It is the capabilities provided by these tools which is facilitating the development of knowledge systems by organizations whose resources and orientation are different than those of the academic world. Benefits of these tools include:

1. Facilitating the knowledge engineers' and domain experts' study of the problem, and its relevant knowledge, reasoning process, and recommendations. Much of this exploration can be achieved without extensive assistance from a skilled programmer.

2. A methodology for explicitly representing this knowledge, reasoning, and recommendation and entering it into an operable system.

3. Provision for various types of reasoning.

4. Interactive graphics for improved understanding.

SHELLS

The expert-system shell, used as a way to develop an expert system by entering information and rules in semi-English format, can be thought of as a high-level language in itself. These systems exist as commercial products in a number of forms and price ranges for nearly all types of computers from PCs to high-end workstations. The idea of a commercial shell first started because in a number of large-scale academic research projects, fairly elaborate programs were written to support the entering of rules and operation of a system that used these rules to perform a useful task. In several, the underlying methodology was extracted from the research project and generalized to provide a ready-made system for development of an expert system. Further, this methodology was then commercialized into a product and sold to those who wished to use it in building their own systems without the need to start from scratch or, in theory, have extensive AI background or experience. There is now a sizeable industry that provides such products on a range of machines.

Most of the original systems were designed for use on one of the high-end LISP machines, primarily because of their power and flexibility. Such machines are relatively expensive at present, and contain many capabilities that may even be undesirable in an operational application. As a result, most shell manufacturers have announced low-cost delivery-system versions of their shells that are programmed in more conventional mainframe or PC languages and can run on such machines.

A related trend is the development and marketing of application-specific shells. Rather than as a tool for developing a broad range of products, tailored shells are now being introduced for use in specific market segments and applications such as finance, manufacturing and diagnosis. These shells permit the shell builder to orient the design of the shell to a specific application type and allow the user, if desired, to incorporate important proprietary features without disclosure outside of the using company.

All the larger shells have powerful development and control logic capability and many of the purchasers of these shells did not have extensive experience with AI at the time of purchase. Thus, of necessity, the manufacturers of these shells found themselves in the training, system support and consulting business as well as selling products. It is likely that these firms will remain sources of such support for some time.

In general, these shells provide excellent support for the early stages of rule and data-intensive prototype development and for the complete life-cycle of systems where "common-sense" behavior is not required. An unsolved problem, at present, for shell manufacturers is the maintenance of mature programs with some "common sense." The "behavior" of a shell-based expert system, from the point of view of the user, is determined by the shell inference engine, the content and order of the input data and the structure and implied control logic of the rules. It is essentially impossible to anticipate all the effective combinations of data and control logic in a large system so that the system, as initially designed and implemented, will occasionally behave unacceptably.

Obviously, to protect their systems from piecemeal copying, and to avoid the need for detailed system maintenance documentation, shell suppliers do not provide source code for their systems. Thus, the addition of "common-sense" behavior to most shells is presently provided by the ability to provide specific control logic at a particular point in the rule structure in the form of appropriate

LISP code that modifies or overrides the normal control logic of the system. Sometimes, it is necessary to use such local control methods to overcome bugs or undesirable processes in the basic shell inference engine. As the system matures and changes and new releases of the shell or the hardware operating system are provided, the effect of these patches is difficult to predict and can result in a considerable unproductive effort, especially since the diagnostic tools provided by the shell manufacturer do not show the effect of these patches. The problem will probably be addressed in future shell designs but it should be considered when estimating development and maintenance requirements for the present generation of shells.

SUPPORT FACILITIES

An important feature of operating systems that are provided with most of the high-end LISP computers is a large repertoire of support tools of various types. Most of these tools were created by AI researchers to assist in the development of large complex programs. The tools permit a skilled programmer to use, with minor modification, a large body of existing code to support new functions. Such processes as the design of user interfaces, file management and graphic displays can be quickly written. Debugging, efficiency testing and incremental compilation routines support rapid analysis and testing of new code. In addition, it is possible to customize all levels of a LISP operating system to meet the needs of an individual programmer.

As opposed to mainframes, most individual AI workstations support the design of user interfaces which are particularly easy to use by a specific group of experts. The Macintosh™ user interface was taken directly from AI user interface concepts and is an example of what can be accomplished. This area of AI has already become a normal part of computer system design. There is much interest in the development of software tools with standardized graphics and user interfaces. Such standards would facilitate the porting of these design capabilities to other machines.

The advent of ever-better tools is decreasing the need for knowledge engineers who are also highly skilled programmers. Tools are being introduced which are specifically intended to aid domain experts in developing their own knowledge systems (Dietz, 1986). In addition to the tools designed to operate on dedicated symbolic processors, many tools are being introduced for workstations and personal computers. In fact, there are so many such tools that it is difficult to select the best tool for a particular application. Selection of a particular tool is a function of the application and, also, the methodology of system implementation. The latter refers to such parameters as how the knowledge is to be represented and the type of logic which is most appropriate. The evaluation and verification of these tools can be time-consuming and inexact. A number of guides are published on an ongoing basis (Harmon and King, 1985).

Although the better software shells and tools do provide numerous aids for the system developer, their effective use may still require substantial investment in training. It is also still frequently necessary to have a skilled programmer available on the development team. Particular applications may require modifying the tool's detailed software coding. The modifications may be necessitated by:

- The inference or representation methodology
- Input/output presentation
- Integration with existing systems
- Improved computation efficiency
- Unwanted behavior under certain conditions

A limitation for some applications is the difficulty of collapsing a system built with the more sophisticated tools into a delivery format. Complex coding modifications may be required in order to delete portions of the system which expedited the development process, but which make run-time execution inefficient.

In order to increase their market potential, some suppliers have implemented their software tools and shells in languages other than LISP or PROLOG. There is considerable interest, for example, in programs written in the C language, particularly for compiled delivery code. These languages may provide some advantages in computation efficiency as well as operation on a wider spectrum of computers. Caution should be exercised, though, on retaining the distinctive features inherent in many knowledge systems. For example, some of these languages obscure the distinction between the knowledge base and the inference engine, thereby losing a major advantage of the AI technology.

There is much interest in software tools and shells which utilize examples to develop knowledge systems, particularly rule-based expert systems. With such a tool a knowledge engineer developing an electronics diagnostics system can incorporate a number of system faults, test procedures, and recommended solutions. When presented with a sufficient number of examples of problems and solutions, the software tool internally sets up the reasoning process. Some successes, particularly in diagnostics, have been recorded. For many applications, however, the capability is still quite limited. There is much current research on improving the capability of these shells (Dolan and Dyer, 1985; Salzberg, 1985).

DELIVERY HARDWARE AND SOFTWARE

For delivery systems, efficiency of the development process is no longer a primary consideration. More important may be:

- Cost effectiveness
- Particular performance features
- User interfaces
- Physical characteristics and environmental requirements
- Support and maintenance facilities
- Connectivity to other hardware and software systems
- Subjective emotions
- Stability across releases and upgrades of the development environment

Any of the above factors can be the overriding consideration in the selection and acquisition of the delivery vehicle.

From the above list it may appear that PCs are the overwhelming choice as a delivery vehicle. While more and more knowledge systems are being delivered on PCs, there are still numerous applications where conventional mainframes and minicomputers are a good choice. For example, some MIS shops have installed knowledge systems on a time-shared mainframe. This provides access to the system for many users, thereby improving the economics of the installation. Where the knowledge system does not require the processing capabilities of a mainframe or dedicated symbolic processor, there is growing interest in using conventional workstations as a delivery vehicle. Particularly attractive is the UNIX environment, which is becoming more widely available on these workstations. The attraction of UNIX in these applications is its portability, ease of integration with other systems, and familiarity. Suppliers of LISP machines are responding by incorporating UNIX environments, and introducing lower-priced machines with improved interfaces to mainframe machines.

The economics and widespread availability of personal computers certainly increases the interest in using them as delivery vehicles for knowledge systems. This is complemented by the fact that there are probably many more application opportunities for small systems that can run on PCs than there are large system applications for the AI technology. Another attraction is that PCs provide a less expensive way to become familiar with AI technology.

Commercially viable systems comprising from 50 to 250 rules can be readily implemented on a PC. This is particularly true if the knowledge base is used primarily to access an external data base. As the rule base becomes larger, operation of the knowledge system on a PC can become unwieldy. It is then sometimes feasible to segment the rules into related groups of 50 or 100. The problem solution and user interface can then be oriented to call up successive segments of expertise. Such an approach, while it has its limits, may be quite satisfactory and cost-effective.

If the knowledge system is to be delivered on many widely dispersed terminals, there are other considerations. Networking to a centralized host machine and data base imposes some technical and performance limitations. There may also be some security concerns about putting proprietary data on a large number of PC delivery vehicles. This problem can be solved by hosting the expert system with its proprietary data on either the mainframe or an attached symbolic processor.

Some software tools and shells which operate on dedicated symbolic processors may also be used on PCs. Since the PC has less processing power, it may be necessary to eliminate some features of the shell such as utilities and sophisticated graphics. The performance as well as user acceptance of PC delivery systems is being increased by writing the knowledge system in widely used languages such as FORTRAN, C, ADA, and Pascal. Advantages of languages such as FORTRAN and C include portability, established data and system integrity, security features, and automatic backup of transactions. Although use of these languages in knowledge systems is becoming more widespread, there is yet no overwhelming preference, particularly for delivery systems.

There is much debate over the relative merits of these languages as compared to LISP and PROLOG. An advantage of LISP-based delivery systems is ease of understanding and access to the knowledge base and inference mechanism. With a LISP system, it may be easier to augment the knowledge base and modify the reasoning procedures.

Applications written in LISP may suffer performance problems at run-time due to inherent overhead. Much of this "excess baggage" is a consequence of the flexibility and power that was so helpful during development. These run-time disadvantages are decreasing with the advent of better compilers and hardware.

SUPPLIERS

Many purchasers of AI equipment, software and services finding it difficult to evaluate alternatives in a competitive situation, ultimately used cost and the total number of features as the important variables. It is certainly true that cost and numbers of features are important in any selection, but such selection methods certainly offer opportunity to motivated vendors to compromise elements of overall system performance at the expense of the unwary.

It may be wise, particularly for the inexperienced buyer, to develop selection criteria in advance, perhaps with experienced outside assistance, before starting the procurement process. It is particularly important to consider the life-cycle cost of the system, including such items as integration, stability, maintenance and the probability that the user will remain satisfied with the performance of a system for a long time.

If outside assistance is used, it is probable that the pertinent experience of the vendor and the personnel assigned to the project is of primary importance, although certain aspects of application design and implementation covered in this book should also be considered when making a selection. If suppliers can describe the process to be used for application design and system development in detail, and provide schedules and benchmarks for the various stages of the process, it is likely that their experience is meaningful. References from several customers of a supplier are likely to be illuminating as well.

Developers of knowledge systems may be faced with a bewildering choice of hardware and software suppliers. Categories of suppliers include:

1. Specialist AI suppliers, many of whom are newcomers.

2. Established mainframe and minicomputer hardware and software vendors.

3. Suppliers of complete packages—financial planning, manufacturing, management, etc. (Such packages may be customized for more specific applications—inventory control, production planning, automotive diagnostics, etc.)

4. Value-added resellers (VAR) are marketing a modification of the packages. Software modules may be bundled with the hardware and marketed as a complete system.

5. Vendors of workstations with augmented capabilities for AI.

6. In-house developers.

7. Universities and government.

8. Developers of custom systems.

As has happened in the case of other emerging technologies, the established market leaders were not initially strong factors in developing and marketing specialized AI hardware.

Because of concern over the possible effect on their existing product line, suppliers of mainframe and minicomputers limit the number of AI-oriented features they will add to their hardware. For example, incorporating symbolic processing architectures can introduce complexities in software compatibility, documentation and support. Eventually, however, perhaps as many as a third of all management information systems will soon have an AI content. Major computer companies will not willingly abandon large portions of their business. Their preference, of course, is to persuade users to develop their AI systems on conventional hardware and software.

Where market pressures indicate that this approach will not completely succeed, many manufacturers of mainframe machines are adding a specialized microprocessor chip to provide some of the symbolic features. This is similar to what is being achieved by adding co-processor chips to conventional hardware. Symbolic processor manufacturers are responding by introducing lower-cost delivery vehicles and increased facility for accessing software modules written in other languages.

The most prominent suppliers of AI development hardware and software have been start-up companies or new operations of existing companies. These suppliers, characterized by an entrepreneurial flair, have been aggressive in developing enhanced products and features. On the negative side, their marketing and support capabilities have sometimes been inadequate. Also, as the actual market for specialized hardware has shrunk, a few have disappeared. But as the total AI market potential increases, so does the competition from suppliers of more conventional hardware and software. These suppliers, who may have a strong existing customer base to protect, have been expanding the capabilities of their systems. Even though the augmented AI features of these machines may be somewhat less than those provided by symbolic processors, they are exerting strong economic pressures upon the marketplace.

Also exerting economic pressures are the suppliers of workstations whose capabilities are being extended to accommodate AI technology requirements. Workstation extensions to AI technology are significant since these workstations are widely accepted as an integral part of engineering design organizations.

The use of AI systems in workstations is currently in considerable flux. There has been fierce competition between the makers of symbolic processors and the makers of workstations. As low-cost processor chips with address word lengths and clock rates in the former super-minicomputer capability range become available, the processing power that can be provided in a low-end workstation is almost equivalent to that of the high-end LISP machines. Most workstation manufacturers are entering into third-party software agreements so that both AI languages and shells are available on these machines. There will probably be increasing use of AI technology in the engineering design area that is the primary marketplace for such machines.

In the area of software tools, there are many new start-up companies. Even the widely recognized software companies providing these tools are small in comparison to computer hardware companies. They may not have the resources to provide the necessary level of training and customer support. However, for well designed and less sophisticated packages, the requirements for training and customer support are minimal.

Other potential suppliers of hardware and software are in-house engineering organizations, custom design houses, and universities. Occasionally, government laboratories also provide prototype hardware and software to their contractors. If the prerequisite technical, cost, and schedule resources are available, in-house development provides several advantages. These may include achieving a competitive advantage, retaining proprietary data, and specializing the design to particular applications. Some of the same advantages can be obtained by using custom design houses, if a satisfactory trade-off can be made on cost and protection of proprietary information. Universities may provide some elements of the hardware and the software system. These elements may be quite advanced technically but severely limited in their applicability to deliverable systems.

14

Experiences

A CASE HISTORY

In numerous presentations that the authors have made on artificial intelligence, many of the questions asked were not of a technical nature. Rather, the questioners were concerned with how an organization could effectively introduce and use this new technology, and what decisions are entailed. These questions came from representatives of a broad range of industries and service organizations. Although posed by individuals of quite different backgrounds, many of the questions were similar. In the belief that an actual example of technology introduction would be of help, this case history is presented.

Litton Industries is a large corporation comprising divisions which provide a diverse range of products and services. Emphasis is placed on making decisions at the division level. There is no corporate headquarters group which mandates the use of a particular technology. There is also no central research facility. Artificial intelligence appeared to be of broad interest to many Litton activities. To determine if this was indeed the case, it was first necessary for corporate decision makers to acquire a basic background in artificial intelligence.

At the corporate level there is a very small group engaged in the study of new technologies and their implications for Litton. As a member of this group, one of the authors became convinced that the potential of AI was sufficient to warrant further study. Convincing higher levels of management was more difficult. There was cynicism and doubt as to what differentiated AI from other computer techniques. Eventually, the president of the corporation approved the expenditure of funds to further evaluate AI. He also insisted that a commitment be made by the operating divisions to insure their serious participation in any study program.

The author was designated the corporate program manager for AI but was told not to proceed with substantial expenditure of funds until he had obtained commitments from a number of operating divisions. Obtaining these commitments entailed many plant visits, presentations, and the convincing of managers that allocation of funds and people to a study of AI would be to their benefit. Occasionally gentle persuasion from corporate headquarters helped. However, a key factor in obtaining division participation was the emergence of an AI proponent who had the technical prowess and appropriate position in the operating division.

A task force was established with representatives from a cross section of Litton businesses, as listed in Figure 14.1. Emphasis was placed on the team members having not only a good background in technology, but also an awareness of how this technology might affect their own division's business. The team members typically had ten to fifteen years of experience. Not all of them were computer specialists; some were middle-level or higher-level technical managers and all were acutely aware of the competitive pressures affecting the success of their organization. Selection as a team member did not automatically generate a high degree of interest in AI. Team members showed considerable cynicism (which proved to be healthy).

At the first meeting, the program manager posed a question to the group, "Should we do anything about AI?" A team member immediately responded, "Is an acceptable answer 'hell no'?" This quickly alerted both the program man-

TASK FORCE

- Airborne Military Electronics
- Machine Tools
- Command and Control Systems
- Software Systems
- Navigation Systems
- Geophysical Exploration
- Optical Systems
- Ship Building
- Communication Systems
- Industrial Automation

Figure 14.1
Businesses Represented on the Task Force

ager and team members to the independent spirit which would prevail throughout the study and evaluations program. (Interestingly, that particular questioner eventually became one of the strongest proponents for introducing AI technology into the company.)

The following objectives were presented to the task force:

1. Comprehend AI's capabilities and limitations.

2. Postulate some preliminary questions and answers: What are the business implications? What is entailed in utilizing AI? What do we do next?

3. Consider in particular the potential of AI to increase the efficiency of internal operations, as a competitive threat, to enhance present products and services, and for developing new business opportunities.

Initially, much of the team's effort was devoted to technical training; learning the concepts and implementation techniques without becoming mired down in research issues. To facilitate this training and to aid in subsequent AI activities, a consulting firm experienced in AI was hired. Current and projected AI capabilities and limitations were studied. Visits to companies who already had some AI development experience were helpful.

As the task force continued to meet, a preponderance of the effort became devoted to consideration of business implications:

- What are the near-term applications of AI?

- What is the potential market?

- Do customers know or care about AI?

- What resources are needed?

- Can a satisfactory return on investment be calculated

Many potential near-term and long-term applications were studied. These applications were then related to potential markets. This proved to be an interesting and useful exercise since the team members typically were not well informed about each other's markets and business environment. Surprisingly, there were a number of problems which were universal to all the representative divisions. Much thought (and heat!) was generated in regard to project pitfalls, schedules, costs, and evaluating return on investment.

A persistent issue concerned how to obtain the technical competence required to develop AI systems. A prevailing company philosophy states that if a given technology is important to an operating division, then that division must develop proficiency in that technology. It was then recognized that trained AI people were very scarce. The recommendation of the team (influenced "naturally" by the fact that the team was composed almost entirely of representatives of operating divisions) was for corporate headquarters to accept the responsibilities and incur the cost of setting up a corporate-wide training program. After several turbulent discussions, it was conceded that setting up a central training facility was not consonant with the corporation's philosophy of decentralized management. Eventually, and reluctantly, it was agreed that it would be preferable for each division to "grow their own" qualified AI personnel. This minimized the structural dislocations which could be caused by hiring expensive, newly minted, AI PhDs. It also placed emphasis on utilizing employees who were already knowledgeable about the division's technology and business. Later experiences demonstrated that these employees could be adequately trained in the design and application of AI systems.

In order to minimize time and cost, the team met at various locations around the country. Attendance was usually good, although there were frequent cases of higher priorities preventing a team member from attending a meeting. The team was fortunate in being invited to discuss AI issues at companies and universities already active in artificial intelligence. As team members became more knowledgeable in the subject, these other companies and institutions welcomed the interchange of ideas.

After about nine months, the team prepared a report which contained some specific conclusions:

1. AI could be used effectively in company operations.

2. The competition was active in AI.

3. The technology provided a vehicle for enhancing present products.

4. AI presented some new business opportunities.

The report was not able to present a quantitative method for calculating return on investment. It was impractical to define an ROI which would be satisfactory for evaluating the wide range of AI applications that were considered. Several members felt that a different yardstick than conventional ROI standards would be required. In spite of the diversity of their backgrounds and differences in business orientation, the team members agreed that AI would be an important factor in their business. Some team members felt that they were already falling behind the competition in using this new technology. Other team members felt that AI would not be important until some time in the future.

The task force's report was presented to division and corporate management. Generally, the report created interest, but not enough to immediately release a flood of financial support for new AI projects. This required a long-term selling effort. Some of the first projects, in fact, were "bootlegged." It was particularly difficult to obtain capital funding for expensive hardware and software that could be used only by one person at a time. Eventually, a few limited-capability prototypes were developed and they became important internal selling tools.

The task force continued to meet, although less regularly. Much of the discussion was taken up with interchanges on how to sell a proposed project to management. Valuable interchanges also took place relating experiences with newly acquired hardware and software. The task force became a focal point for initiating corporate-wide purchasing agreements. It continued to provide a good forum for supplier presentations and was effective in arranging visits to other organizations active in AI. One of the most valuable outgrowths of the task force was establishment of an informal communications network between task force participants. Normally, since they were from divisions engaged in quite different businesses, the team members might have had little occasion to discuss common problems with each other. Although the makeup of the team has changed somewhat, this informal network continues (as of 1987) to be useful, particularly in sharing experiences.

There is no longer a great need to convince various levels of management that AI is "for real." The technology is considered for its benefits as are other technologies. A number of AI projects have been successfully undertaken. The task force continues to meet, although on a less regular basis and with some new members. It succeeded in its mission of evaluating AI and employing it where appropriate.

REFLECTIONS

Decision makers concerned with implementing or using AI technology may be confronted with factors which differ from their previous experience. After sifting through the hyperbole and conflicting emotions, they generally agree that it is obvious there is something of substance in AI technology. Although there may be variations in the timetable, this technology will be pervasive in providing many products and services.

The decision maker is confronted with both similarities and differences to other new programs. The elements of good project management are applicable as are marketing considerations. A frustration is the difficulty in determining an appropriate return on investment, particularly for projects entailing a substantial commitment of resources. AI deals with uncertainty and this can be unsettling. There are new participants in the market and new strategic alliances are being formed. Social and legal implications of using this technology may be uncertain.

Benefits of utilizing artificial intelligence technology are great enough to initiate resolution of these nagging doubts. The decision maker must react accordingly.

Appendix I

References

Chapter 1. History and Role

Barr, A. and E. Feigenbaum, 1981, *Handbook of Artificial Intelligence*, William Kaufman.

Chapter 2. Potential for Artificial Intelligence

Anonymous, 1986, "An intelligent way to develop software," *Information Week,* June 23.

Anonymous, 1987, "The Outlook," *Wall Street Journal,* Page 1, February 9.

Bimson, K. D. and L. B. Burris, 1986, "Knowledge representation in software project management: Theory and practice," Forum on Artificial Intelligence in Management, May.

Boden, M. A., 1985, "Panel: Artificial intelligence and legal responsibility," *Proceedings,* Ninth International Joint Conference of Artificial Intelligence.

Bruno, G., A. Elia, and P. LaPace, 1986, "A rule-based system to schedule production," Computer Society of IEEE, July.

Chace, W. M., 1985, "Intelligence, artificial and otherwise," *The AI Magazine,* Winter issue.

Dickson, E. M., 1985, "Comparing artificial intelligence and genetic engineering," *The AI Magazine,* Winter issue.

Faught, W. S., 1986, "Application of AI in engineering," *IEEE Computer,* July.

Gandchi, J. M. and J. A. Gandchi, 1985, "Intelligent tools: The cornerstone of a new civilization," *The AI Magazine,* Fall issue.

Hayes-Roth, F., 1984, "The machine as a partner of the new professional," *IEEE Spectrum,* June.

Jordan, J. A., Jr., 1986, "Impact of AI on management—insights from the EWIM consultant," Forum of Artificial Intelligence in Management, May.

Kinoglu, F., D. Riley and M. Donath, 1986, "Artificial intelligence: Expert system model of the design process,"*Design News,* March 3.

Mittal, S., C. L. Dym, and M. Morjaria, 1986, "PRIDE: An expert system for the design of paper handling systems," *IEEE Computer,* July.

Mishelevich, D. J., 1985, "Commercial viability of AI in medicine: How and when," First Annual Artificial Intelligence and Advanced Computer Technology Conference.

Nilsson, N. J., 1984, "Artificial intelligence: Employment and income," *The AI Magazine,* Summer issue.

Piatetsky-Shapiro, G., G. Jakobson, C. Lamford and E. Nyberg, 1986, "An intelligent database assistant," *IEEE Expert,* Summer issue.

Seeley, L. N., P. Chapman and M. A. Levzinger, 1986, "Experimental database applications using natural language processing," *Proceedings,* Westex-86, Computer Society of IEEE, June.

Smith, S. F. and P. Owi, 1986, "Integrating multiple scheduling perspectives to generate detailed production schedules," Society of Manufacturing Engineers, Ultratech Conference, September.

Sprowl, J., K. Applegate, M. Evans, H. Harr and R. Rueb, 1986, "Human interfaces in a legal expert system," AFIPS *Proceedings,* Vol. 55, 1986 National Computer Conference.

Tenant, H., 1986, "Tomorrow's desktops: Changing the way people work," *Computer Design,* July.

Whalen, P. J. and T. F. Skoronski, 1986, "DOSS—An expert system for large scale design," SPIE, Vol. 635, *Application of Artificial Intelligence III,* April.

Wolfe, A., 1986, "Software productivity moves upstream, *Electronics,* July 10.

Chapter 3. Applications

Anonymous, 1986, "Ultratech Conference," Society of Manufacturing Engineers, September.

Bangs, E. R., 1986, "AI in the development of adaptive controls in fusion welding," Society of Manufacturing Engineers, Ultratech Conference.

Bonissone, P. P., 1983, "DELTA: An expert system to troubleshoot diesel electric locomotives," *Proceedings,* ACM, October.

Chandrasekaren, B., and J. W. Smith, 1985, "Tenth annual workshop on artificial intelligence in medicine," *The AI Magazine,* Summer issue.

Drogin, E. M., 1986, "AI issues for realtime systems," *Defense Electronics,* June.

Forbus, K. D., 1986, "Interpreting measurements of physical systems," *Proceedings,* AAAI-86, August.

Harandi, M. T. and M. D. Lubars, 1986, "Knowledge-based software development: A paradigm and a tool," AFIPS *Proceedings,* Vol. 55, 1986 National Computer Conference.

Harmon, P., 1986, "Expert systems in use today," *Expert Systems Strategies* (Newsletter), August.

Hewett, J. and R. Sasson, 1986, *Expert Systems 1986, Vol. 1: USA and Canada;* Ovum Ltd.

Neilson, N. T., 1986, "Knowledge-based simulation programming," AFIPS *Proceedings,* Vol. 55, 1986 National Computer Conference.

Schmolze, J. C., 1986, "Physics for robots," *Proceedings,* AAAI-86, August.

Taylor, W. A., 1986, "Artificial intelligence: Potentials and limitations," *Design News,* March 3.

Walker, T. C. and R. K. Miller, 1986, "Expert systems 1986: An assessment of technology and applications," SEAI *Technical Publications.*

Chapter 4. Artificial Intelligence Concepts

Anonymous, 1984–1985, "ICOT journals and digests," Institute for New Generation Computer Technology.

Anonymous, 1986, "Optoelectronics builds viable neural-net memory," *Electronics,* June 16.

Barr, A. and E. Feigenbaum, 1981, *Handbook of Artificial Intelligence,* William Kaufman.

Bock, P., 1986, "Emergence of artificial intelligence: Learning to learn," *The AI Magazine,* Fall issue.

Charniak, E. and D. McDermott, 1984, *Introduction to Artificial Intelligence,* Addison-Wesley.

Chien, S. A., 1987, "Extending explanation-based learning: Failure-driven schema refinement," *Proceedings,* Third Conference on Artificial Intelligence Applications, Computer Society of IEEE, February.

Colmerauer, A., H. Kanoui and M. Van Canegham, 1981, "Last steps towards an ultimate PROLOG," *Proceedings,* International Joint Conference on Artificial Intelligence (IJCAI-81), August.

Davis, D. B., 1981, "Artificial intelligence goes to work," *High Technology,* April.

Dechter, R., and D. Michie, 1984, *Structured Induction of Plans and Programs,* IBM Los Angeles Scientific Center, November.

DeKleer, J. and J. Seeley-Brown, 1984, "A qualitative physics based on confluences," *Artificial Intelligence,* Vol. 24.

Dolan, C. and M. Dyer, 1985, "Learning planning heuristics through observations," *Proceedings,* Ninth International Joint Conference on Artificial Intelligence.

Dreyfus, H. and S. Dreyfus, 1986, "Why expert systems do not exhibit expertise," *IEEE Expert,* Summer issue.

Elliot, L. B., 1986, "Analogical problem solving and expert systems," *IEEE Expert,* Summer issue.

Gayle, B. G. and D. D. Dankel, 1986, "RxPert: An intelligent computer system for drug interactions," SPIE, Vol. 635, *Applications of Artificial Intelligence III,* April.

Green, P. E., 1985, "Resource limitations issues in realtime intelligent systems," SPIE, Vol. 635, *Applications of Artificial Intelligence III,* April.

Handle, S. and H. M. Hastings, 1986, "Computer simulates brain architecture," *Applied Artificial Intelligence Reporter,* May.

Hayes-Roth, F., D. A. Waterman and D. B. Lenat, 1983, *Building Expert Systems,* Addison-Wesley.

Lenat, D. B., n.d., "An artificial intelligence approach to discovery in mathematics of heuristic search," *Memo* AIM 286, Department of Computer Sciences, Stanford University, Stanford, California.

Lenat, D. B., 1983, "EURISKO: A program that learns new heuristics and domain concepts, Nature of Heuristics III; Program Design and Results," *Artificial Intelligence,* Vol. 21.

Lenat, D. B. and J. S. Brown, 1984, "Why AM and EURISKO appear to work," *AI Journal,* Vol. 23, August.

McDermott, D., Waldrop, M. M., R. Shank, B. Chandrasekaran, and J. McDermott, 1985, "The dark ages of AI," *The AI Magazine,* Fall issue.

Neves, D. M., 1985, "Learning procedures from examples and by doing," *Proceedings,* Ninth International Joint Conference on Artificial Intelligence.

Pazzani, M. J., 1986, "Refining the knowledge base of a diagnostic expert system: An application of failure driven learning," *Proceedings,* AAAI-86, August.

Port, O., 1986, "Computers that come awfully close to thinking," *Business Week,* June 2.

Raulefs, P., B. D'Ambrosio, M. Fehling, S. Forrest and M. Wilber, 1987, "Realtime process management for materials composition," *Proceedings,* Third Conference on Artificial Intelligence Applications, Computer Society of IEEE, February.

Ritchie, G. D. and F. K. Hanna, 1984, "AM: A case study in AI methodology," *Artificial Intelligence,* Vol. 23, No. 3, August.

Salzberg, S., 1985, "Heuristics for inductive learning," *Proceedings,* Ninth International Joint Conference on Artificial Intelligence.

Steele G. L., Jr., 1984, *Common LISP—The Language,* Digital Press.

Turban, E. and P. R. Watkins, 1986, "Integrating expert systems and decision support systems," Forum on Artificial Intelligence in Management, May.

Waterman, D. A., 1986, *A Guide to Expert Systems,* Addison-Wesley.

Williamson, M., 1987, "DuPont uses PCs for AI implementation," *PC Week,* January 13.

Winegard, T., R. Davis, S. Dreyfus and B. Smith, 1985, "Expert systems: How far can they go?", *Proceedings,* Ninth International Joint Conference on Artificial Intelligence.

Winston, P. H., 1984, *Artificial Intelligence,* Second Edition, Addison-Wesley.

Chapter 5. The Market for Artificial Intelligence

Inverson, W. R., 1987, "NCR sees its edge in systems expertise," *Electronics,* April 2.

Schorr, H., 1986, "AI: The second wave," *Proceedings,* Fifth National Conference on Artificial Intelligence, AAAI-86, August.

Chapter 6. Investment Decisions

Kautz, H. A. and J. F. Allen, 1986, "Generalized plan recognition," *Proceedings,* AAAI-86, August.

Chapter 7. Knowledge and Its Management

Kidder, T., 1985, *House,* Avon.

Pearl, J., 1983, "Knowledge versus search: A quantitative analysis using A*", *Artificial Intelligence,* Vol. 20, 70.1.

Sacks, O., 1985, *The Man Who Mistook His Wife for a Hat,* Harper and Rowe.

Spradley, J., 1979, *The Ethnographic Interview,* Holt, Rinehart and Winston.

Waterman, D. A., 1986, *A Guide to Expert Systems,* Addison-Wesley.

Chapter 8. Selecting an Appropriate Project

Naffah, N., G. White and S. Gibbs, 1986, "Design issues of an intelligent workstation for the office," AFIPS *Proceedings,* Vol. 55, 1986 Computer Conference.

Prerau, D. S., 1985, "Selection of an appropriate domain for an expert system," *The AI Magazine,* Summer issue.

Schaeffer, J. and T. A. Marsland, 1985, "Utility of expert knowledge," *Proceedings,* Ninth International Joint Conference on Artificial Intelligence.

Chapter 9. Selling the Project

Fried, L., 1986, "Commercial uses of expert systems in U.S. corporations," Forum on Artificial Intelligence in Management, May.

Chapter 10. Who Designs the System?

Akey, M. L. and K. A. Dunkelberger, 1987, "Building near-term military systems: Formalisms and an example," *Proceedings*, Third Conference on Artificial Intelligence Applications, Computer Society of IEEE, February.

Kowalik, J. S., 1985, "AI technology transfer program at Boeing," First Annual Artificial Intelligence and Computer Technology Conference.

Schindler, P. 1986, "AI is becoming just another form of DP," *Information Week,* May 5.

Warn, K., 1986, "DORIS—A case study in expert systems shell development," Society of Manufacturing Engineers, Ultratech Conference, September.

Chapter 11. Project Organization and Management

Anonymous, 1986, "Expert systems in the workplace," *Datamation,* January.

Bachant, J. and J. McDermott, 1984, "R1 revisited: Four years in the trenches," *The AI Magazine,* Fall issue.

Harmon, P., 1986, *Expert Systems Strategies* (Newsletter) January.

Hayes-Roth, F., D. A. Waterman and D. B. Lenat, 1983, *Building Expert Systems,* Addison-Wesley.

Mittal, S., 1985, "Knowledge acquisition from multiple experts," *The AI Magazine,* Summer issue.

Smith, R. G., 1984, "On the development of commercial expert systems," *The AI Magazine,* Fall issue.

Waterman, D. A., 1986, *A Guide to Expert Systems,* Addison-Wesley.

Chapter 12. Implementing the Project

Bouwman, M. J., 1983, "Human diagnostic reasoning by computer: An illustration from financial analysis," *Management Science,* Vol. 29, No. 6, June.

Freedman, R. S. and J. P. Rosenking, 1986, "Designing computer-based systems: OBIE-1: KNOBE," *IEEE Expert,* Summer issue.

Hayes-Roth, F., D. A. Waterman and D. B. Lenat, 1983, *Building Expert Systems,* Addison-Wesley.

Hollan, J. D., E. L. Hutchins and L. Weitzman, 1984, "STEAMER: An interactive inspectable simulation-based training system," *The AI Magazine,* Summer issue.

Kline, P. J. and S. B. Dolins, 1986, "Moving from problems to expert systems solutions," *Proceedings,* Westrex '86, Computer Society of IEEE, June.

Kosy, D. W., 1986, "Experiments with self-explanatory financial planning models," Forum on Artificial Intelligence in Management, May.

McKeowin, K. R., M. Wish and K. Mathews, 1985, "Tailoring explanations for the user," *Proceedings,* Ninth International Joint Conference on Artificial Intelligence.

Neches, R., W. R. Swartout and J. Moore, 1985, "Explainable (and maintainable) expert systems," *Proceedings,* Ninth International Joint Conference on Artificial Intelligence.

Nguyen, T. A., W. A. Perkins, T. J. Laffey and D. Pecora, 1985, "Checking an expert system's knowledge base for consistency and completeness," *Proceedings,* Ninth International Joint Conference on Artificial Intelligence.

Powell, C. A., C. K. Pickering and K. T. Westcourt, 1986, "System integration of knowledge-based maintenance aids," *Proceedings,* AAAI-86, August.

Semeco, A. C., B. D. Williams, S. Roth and J. F. Gilmore, 1986, "Gensched—A real world hierarchical planning knowledge-based system," SPIE, Vol. 635, *Applications of Artificial Intelligence III,* April.

Vilnat, A. and G. Sabah, 1985, "Be brief, be to the point. . .be seated, or relevant responses in man/machine conversation," *Proceedings,* Ninth International Joint Conference on Artificial Intelligence.

Chapter 13. Hardware and Software

Davis, D. V., 1986, "Artificial intelligence enters the mainstream," *High Technology,* July.

Dietz, P. W., 1986, "Artificial intelligence: Building rule-based expert systems," *Design News,* March 3.

Dolan, C .and M. Dyer, 1985, "Learning planning heuristics through observations," *Proceedings,* Ninth International Joint Conference on Artificial Intelligence.

Harmon, P. and D. King, 1985, "Expert systems—Artificial intelligence in business," John Wiley and Sons.

Hewett, J. and R. Sasson, 1986, *Expert Systems 1986—Volume 1: U.S.A. and Canada,* Ovum Ltd.

Highberger, D. and D. Edson, 1984, "Intelligent computing era takes off," *Computer Design,* September.

Salzberg, S., 1985, "Heuristics for inductive learning," *Proceedings, Ninth International Joint Conference on Artificial Intelligence.*

Verity, J. W., 1986, "The LISP race heats up," *Datamation,* August.

Glossary

algorithmic logic Formula-based logic where meaning is expressed in numerical terms and the order of operations can be predicted in advance. Most conventional computer programs use algorithmic logic.

artificial intelligence (AI) A field of computer science that has as its prime focus the modeling of human behavior with computer programs. The field covers both the development of theories of brain or mind functioning and advanced computer technology to implement the implications of these theories.

backward chaining One of several methods used in an inference engine (which see) to select and operate on components of a knowledge base. An example of backward chaining can be shown with a series of procedural rules of the form IF *x* THEN *y*; where *x* is a condition and *y* is a result. When backward chaining is used, the system would start with a possible result, of the form *y* and look for a rule or combination of rules that has or generates the specific result *y*.

blackboard/blackboard architecture An expert system design in which a single working memory or data base, the blackboard, is accessed by any of several cooperating expert subsystems. Typically, the blackboard is designed to handle hypotheses at different levels of abstraction or to mediate activities of the subsystems.

computer-aided design/computer-aided manufacturing (CAD/ CAM) A computer-based software system that will assist an engineer or draftsman in the design and manufacturing process. A CAD/CAM system replaces much of the hand labor required to prepare a working drawing of a part and the instructions describing how it is to be manufactured.

causal reasoning A knowledge representation technique which attempts to represent causal relationships between events or conditions in the physical world. Causal relationships are generally based on facts or theories, although they may be represented qualitatively or even crudely. The causal relationships serve as an organizing principle for the control structure and make it possible for a system to provide meaningful explanations of its reasoning.

combinatorial growth/explosion Many AI programs require the testing of a large number of alternatives. If care is not taken in the design of the search strategy through these alternatives, the number of combinations to be tested will grow so large as to be impractical to test, i.e., the program would virtually take forever to run under some circumstances.

command language A term used to describe the language that would be employed by a user of a computer program to operate that program as opposed to the code or language in which the program was written.

connectivity The ability to effectively communicate information between different hardware and software systems.

context The situation under which a particular piece of knowledge is applicable or used. Recognition of context is a natural form of human intelligence. It has proved difficult to implement in a computer program unless tight control is provided by the system developer. Accurate context recognition has proved to be a difficult problem for natural language systems.

decision rules One of several terms used to describe the procedures that are included in many expert systems. (If this is true, then do that.)

decision support systems Computer programs based on various deterministic or probabilistic optimization methods used in managerial decision making.

decision tree A hierarchical structure of alternative actions showing the relationships between selection of one alternative and the availability of subsequent alternatives.

deep reasoning See causal reasoning.

degrees of freedom (robotics) The number of axes in which a system can move. A simple placement system may have only three degrees of freedom. A fully articulated robot arm may have as many as nine.

delivery system Generally refers to the computer hardware and operating system used to support the operational version of a computer program. In most cases, the expensive and complex capabilities that assist a programmer in rapid and efficient programming are omitted as unnecessary.

development environment Refers to the computer hardware, operating system and development support software that assist a qualified programmer in rapid and efficient code development. Tools like editors, debuggers, and performance monitors are provided.

diagnostic system A system that, when provided with observations, measurements and test results, can determine the cause of problems or failure. Many expert diagnostic systems will conduct a structured dialog with a user that will lead to the cause of a problem with a minimum of measurement and testing.

domain expert An individual with detailed knowledge about a particular area or field.

embedded AI Refers to the use of AI hardware and software within a larger system based on conventional hardware and software.

embedded control In applications where the rules are context-dependent, it may be necessary to provide local control functions for specific sets of rules, rather than relying on a single inference engine.

error recovery The mechanisms that should be provided in a computer program to assist the user of the program in recovering from the effect of improper use or data.

experiential Based on experience.

expert system A term originally used to describe a computer program that could replace at least some aspect of the normal performance of a human expert. Subsequently used to describe a system that is based on procedural rules or was built with the use of one of many tools or shells designed for the purpose.

firmware Refers to the use of computer circuitry that contains the equivalent of a software program. The program elements are basically prewired.

flow of logical control In a procedural rule-based system, it is often the case that more than one rule will be satisfied when a new fact is entered. The flow of control is the process in the inference engine that selects the order in which the rules are acted upon.

firing rules Jargon for the action where the conditions of a rule are met and the action described in the rule takes place.

frames/frame oriented A representation technique in which objects are associated with a set of attributes, characteristics or features. In some systems, frames may be organized hierarchically with the possibility of inheritance down the hierarchy.

functional specification A description of the processes to be implemented in a computer program.

fuzzy logic A knowledge representation technique designed to codify information that is approximate or imprecise. The logic calculus is designed to handle not only the truth values "true" and "false," but also intermediate values such as "sometimes true" and "seldom true."

garbage collection As a LISP program executes in a computer, memory locations are assigned to temporary or permanent data items by the operating system. Eventually, this assignment process would consume all the available memory. The garbage collection system tests each memory location assignment to see if it is still valid and, if not, returns the unneeded memory to a state where it can be reused.

high-level language A language where some of the design and implementation functions are provided automatically by the compiler rather than manually by the programmer.

high-end AI development tools Software packages which facilitate the acquisition, representation and manipulation of knowledge used in large-scale AI systems. These tools include, among others, incremental compilers, help systems that understand the syntax of the language with which they are used, debuggers, powerful editors, and performance monitors.

high-end development environment Combination of a powerful, single-user computer with extensive graphics capability and appropriate high-end development tools. The development environment is intended to aid in the analysis, design, coding, and debugging of large AI systems.

high-end machines The powerful single-user computers used in high-end development environments. These systems may have specialized architecture and software, provide high-speed operation with large memory capacity, and offer extensive input-output capabilities.

high-power workstations Single-user computers with computing power equivalent to a super-minicomputer. These computers include hardware and software for use in designing complex systems. Some systems may be an augmentation of a conventional engineering work-station including a capability to use AI technology.

inference engine   That component of a knowledge-based system which provides the primary reasoning and control strategies used to operate the system. Trade jargon occasionally has them "inferencing."

knowledge elicitation   The process of identifying and obtaining knowledge. This process usually includes detailed, focused interviews with experts who possess and use the identified knowledge.

knowledge engineering   This term has a range of meaning among different AI groups. At one extreme, knowledge engineering is consid-ered to be the activity associated with eliciting and modeling the knowledge and reasoning strategies of an expert as a basis for the development of a computer program. At the other extreme, knowledge engineering is considered to be the programming of rules in an expert system.

knowledge model   A structured representation of a body of knowl-edge. Although a knowledge model is generally developed for the purpose of serving as the knowledge and reasoning basis for an expert system, it can exist independently of any computer system and may have value by itself as a codification of previously inaccessible knowl-edge.

knowledge representation   The methods and techniques used to model and encode facts and relationships in a knowledge base.

knowledge system   A system with more modest goals than those that have been described for the "expert system." A knowledge system can be based on the use of selected elements of human knowledge rather than on the modeling or replacement of a human expert. By this definition, most "expert" systems are actually knowledge systems.

knowledge worker   Someone whose job functions include judgments and reasoning from data.

life-cycle cost The total cost for development, implementation, operation, upgrading and maintenance of a computer program or other system over the entire time the system will be developed and used.

machine vision   That body of technology that provides a capability for image-based sensing in the control of robotic systems.

menu-based The design of a user interface that supports a command language based on the selection of items from a menu. This approach makes it easier for the designer of the system to be sure that user commands are given in the proper context.

natural language   An area of AI research which concentrates on enabling computers to correctly interpret input typed in a natural human language, such as English, instead of a cryptic, computer command language.

neural networks An area of AI research concentrating on development of computers with many thousands of processors that are highly interconnected and capable of parallel processing. Also known as connectionism and neurocomputing, neural networking is inspired by theoretical models of how the human brain works.

operating system   A computer program which provides the basic operations of computing such as file, read, save, and print.

parallel computing The use of multiple processors in an architecture that permits the processors to perform multiple tasks that may or may not be interdependent.

pattern matching   Selecting an item on the basis of similarity to another item. Because most computers are ultimately based on the use of binary numbers, computer pattern matching is comparison of binary number strings.

porting Transferring a computer program from one type of computer to another. Generally used when there is sufficient difference between the computers that the program must be modified. The ability to so port (transfer) programs is a measure of compatibility, not the ambiguous "portability."

primitive computer operation   Refers to the lowest level of operations in a computer. Examples would be add, shift, jump.

procedural rules   Rules which represent direct control over the sequential operations in a computer program.

production rules   An expression of a conditional relationship, usually of the form: IF [condition] THEN [action].

prototype   A computer program that has not been completed to fully operational status but is sufficiently functional that its operation can be demonstrated.

pruning   The term is applied to a procedure for reducing the time and computing resources required for a search. Methods that evaluate the cost and possible benefit of continuing the examination of a particular set of alternatives are used to decide whether to stop or continue.

rapid prototyping   Jargon for the use of programming methods that speed up the process of coding. Less attention is give to specification, documentation and complete debugging. Used to produce a prototype or demonstration system.

realtime operation   Using a computer program under conditions where its speed of operation does not limit the behavior of an external process.

recursive   A characteristic of a function or procedure, possible in certain programming languages, of calling or using itself. Recursive functions are particularly useful for searching or manipulating tree structures.

representation methods/structure   The techniques or scheme for representing facts and the relationships between facts in a form suitable for incorporation in a computer program.

robotics That part of computer technology that provides sensing and control capability needed for use of robots in industrial applications.

rule An expression of a relationship between facts or condition-action pairs in the form IF [fact 1] THEN [action] or IF [condition] THEN [action].

rule-based system A computer program in which knowledge is represented mainly in the form of rules.

scenarios/scripts Knowledge-representation techniques for representing events that occur in sequence over time.

scene segmentation The division of the output of a robotic vision system into areas of similarity. The division is performed with the use of algorithms that can analyze the scene for texture, intensity, edges, etc.

semantic nets A knowledge-representation technique in which objects or concepts are represented by nodes, and links between the nodes represent the relationships between the objects or concepts.

shallow reasoning As opposed to deep reasoning (see causal reasoning), a reasoning model based mainly on direct condition-action pairs with few inferred conditions between initial data and resulting action.

shells A term used to describe a software system that can assist in the building of an AI system, particularly one using procedural rules.

speech understanding An area of AI research which concentrates on enabling computers to accept audio input from a microphone, recognizing the signals as a meaningful string of words.

symbolic processing The use of logical operations to manipulate data as opposed to the use of numeric processes.

truth maintenance A field of AI research concerned with the use of data whose value may change over time. When such changes occur, previous results may become invalid and need correction.

tuning Jargon for increasing the efficiency or speed of operation of a computer program by rewriting parts of the software that take excessive amounts of time to run or are used frequently.

validation The formal process of testing a computer program to be sure that it meets the design requirements given for its development, usually by test cases or other prespecified procedures.

verification The process of proving that the operation of a computer program does not generate errors or problems, usually by operating it in an environment similar to that in which it will be eventually used. The performance and results must conform to the expectations of the developer and user.

VSLI Very Large Scale Integration is concerned with the development of integrated circuits on single chips that contain very large numbers of transistors. Their manufacture entails solution of problems of layout, and fault-free manufacture of micron-sized components.

XCON Expert Configurator of VAX 11/780 Computer Systems, an expert system developed by Digital Equipment Corporation in collaboration with Carnegie-Mellon University's Computer Science Department during the early 1980s. The reported benefits of XCON in improving accuracy of order-filling, increasing order-filling throughput, reducing inventory and space rquirements and redistributing highly skilled personnel have had a strong positive effect on the acceptance of AI technology by business leaders.

Index